Ex-Spouses and New Spouses: A Study of Relationships

CONTEMPORARY STUDIES IN SOCIOLOGY, VOLUME 7

CONTEMPORARY STUDIES IN SOCIOLOGY
Theoretical and Empirical Monographs

Ex-Spouses and New Spouses: A Study of Relationships

by ANNE-MARIE AMBERT

Department of Sociology
York University

 **JAI PRESS INC.**

Greenwich, Connecticut *London, England*

Library of Congress Cataloging-in-Publication Data
Ambert, Anne-Marie, 1940-
    Ex-spouses and new spouses.

    (Contemporary studies in sociology ; v. 7)
    Bibliography: p,
    Includes index.
    1. Divorced people--Ontario--Toronto Metropolitan
Area--Longitudinal studies. 2. Remarriage--Ontario--
Toronto Metropolitan Area--Longitudinal studies.
I. Title.   II. Series.
HQ840.T67A47   1989   306.89   89-15220
ISBN 1-55938-064-0

CONTENTS

List of Tables

Acknowledgments

This project was sponsered by a Leave Fellowship from the Social Sciences and Humanities Research Council of Canada, 1984-1985, as well as by two research grants from the Faculty of Arts, York University, 1984-1985, 1985-1986.

Sections of Chapter III, "Relationship Between Ex-Spouses," were published in Ambert, A.-M., "Relationship Between Ex-Spouses: Individual and Dyadic Perspectives," *Journal of Social and Personal Reltionships* 5 (August 1988): 327-346 (Copyright © 1988 by Sage Publications, 28 Banner Street, London EC1Y 8QE. Reprinted with permission). Also, and abbreviated version of Chapter VII, "The New Spouses and Their Stepparenting Experience," appeared in Ambert, A.-M., "Being a Stepparent: Live-in and Visiting Children," *Journal of Marriage and the Family* 48 (November 1986): 795-804 (Copyrighted ©1986 by the National Council on Family Relations, 1910 West Country Road B, Suite 147, St. Paul, Minnesota 55113. Reprinted with permission). I wish to thank John Peters who commented on an earlier draft of the chapter on age differences. I have also appreciated the feedback received during a colloquium at the Medical Psychology Unit of the University of Cambridge under the sponsorship of M.P.M. Richards. Suzanne de Leeuw's expert wordprocessing of draft after draft is gratefully acknowledged.

Above all, my gratitude goes to the 252 respondents who gave generously of their time and shared the essence of their lives with me—many three times over a period of six years. I hope this book reflects as accurately as possible what they have expressed in the interviews.

Anne-Marie Ambert

Chapter I

Overview

This book has a dual focus. First, the relationship that ex- spouses develop after their separation, divorce, and remarriage is explored. How do they get along? How do they coparent? How do they perceive their past marital happiness? The other focus is on the remarriage, that is, the current spouses. The relationship that these various persons have forged is also examined; that is, ex-spouses, new spouses, ex-spouses' new spouses—the network approach.

Studies of marriage are generally carried out by interviewing or giving a questionnaire to *one* spouse, more often than not the wife. Relatively few studies include *both* spouses and even fewer look at both partners *together* so as to study couples. A truly dyadic study has to compare the answer of each wife with those of her husband and of each ex-wife with those of her ex- husband. This book presents both the individual perspective and the couple (for remarriage) as well as the ex-couple (for divorce) perspective; moreover, in instances of multiple divorces, the point of view of all the ex-partners involved. This approach is a unique contribution to the study of divorce and remarriage.

After Chapter II describes how the research was carried out, there are two chapters devoted to the ex-dyads. Chapter III examines how ex-husbands and ex-wives get along and how they feel about each other. Case vignettes of ex-couples are presented so as to illustrate a wide range of post-marital relationships. Chapter IV examines how these ex-husbands and ex-wives evaluate their past marriage to each other. Because a surprising number of divorced persons believe their previous marriage to have been a happy one, we will

1

ask: Why did they divorce? Case studies of ex-couples who had been unhappy are presented as a contrast both to those who had been happy and to those couples where only one spouse had been happy.

However, this is only one part of Chapter IV. The other part focuses on remarried couples and their evaluation of their current marriage. The marital happiness in previous marriages is contrasted with the happiness of the *same persons* in their current marriages. Consequently, Chapter IV is also the first of three chapters focusing on remarriage: the others are Chapters VI and VII.

The focus of Chapter V is on multiply-divorced persons and their ex-spouses. This chapter provides an overview on persons who divorce repeatedly; this perspective is given by all their ex-spouses, and even their current one. It is a triadic and even a quadratic approach. Are the multiply-divorced different from the once-divorced? Are their ex-spouses different from the ex-spouses of the once-divorced? Do they tend to remarry the same type of persons? These are some of the questions explored.

Chapter VI addresses a neglected area: age differences in remarriage. Indeed, a majority of remarriages involve partners with much larger age differences than is the case in first marriages. What are the consequences for marital stability and marital happiness when two persons who are at different life stages marry each other? Do particular complications arise? Are both partners equally satisfied?

Chapter VII examines the remarried respondents' stepparenting experience. I was especially interested in exploring whether there were differences in stepparents' happiness depending on the place of residence of the stepchildren. Therefore, persons with live-in stepchildren are compared to persons whose stepchildren are on their own, and to persons whose stepchildren live with the other parent. Chapter VII also explores possible differences between stepmothers and stepfathers in terms of marital happiness and attachment to stepchildren.

Having examined various aspects of the relationship between former spouses and between the new spouses of a remarriage, Chapter VIII asks: When a woman marries a formerly-divorced man, what kind of relationship does she have with *his* ex-wife? What kind of a relationship does a man have with his ex-wife's new husband? Are networks established between these various persons?

Most of the information presented in this book results from interviews carried out in 1984. However, as this study spanned a 6-year period, I will occasionally present information gathered in the previous interviews in 1981 and 1978 respectively. At times, especially in Chapter IX, I refer to results reported on in analyses of data not included in the current book. A list of the publications and reports on complementary topics and analyses from this study is presented in the references.

Chapter II

Description of the Study

I don't care how the computer printout will describe me; statistics go one way and I go the other. The fact that I am divorced has little bearing on who I am and what I am.

—Woman, professional

Am glad I can explain my answers to you because a yes or a no is not enough for me.

—Man, skilled worker

What you've got to do with this [the interview material] now is to write a book, and say it the way it really is—I couldn't afford a divorce but that's all I got in life, a lousy piece of paper that gives me no rights and all the burdens in the world.

—Custodial mother on welfare

This study was carried out in three phases: interviews were first conducted in 1978-1980 (Time 1), then in 1981 (Time 2), and again in 1984 (Time 3). The first four sections in this chapter describe the sample and the processes involved in its selection. The subsequent sections (1) deal with the problems inherent to most studies of divorce as a result of the fact that few take social class into consideration, (2) detail the goals of each wave of interviews and the methods used in gathering the information that is the basis of this book, and (3) include a discussion on the difficulties involved in obtaining truly random samples in the study of divorce and remarriage. The final section discusses the merits of studies such as this one where the researcher takes an active role in gathering the data in contrast to studies wherein researchers use

5

second-hand data from public surveys and never meet the human beings who constitute their data base.

DESCRIPTION OF INITIAL SAMPLE

Between October 1978 and mid-1980, 49 persons who were separated or divorced were interviewed in metropolitan Toronto. The 26 women and 23 men had been separated for an average of two years—the women had been separated a little over two years while the men had been for a little less than two years. Twenty women were custodial mothers and six were childless; they ranged in age from 23 to 48. Seven of the men were custodial fathers, 10 were noncustodial fathers, and six were childless; they ranged in age from 28 to 46.

The last six months during Time 1 were spent attempting to locate custodial fathers of all social strata. Not only was it impossible to obtain a large number of custodial fathers via the referral or snowball method, it was equally impossible to locate more than one father at the lower end of the socioeconomic scale (Ambert 1982a). This problem is not unusual because several other researchers (e.g., Arnold et al. 1980; Defrain and Eirick 1981; Orthner et al. 1976) have experienced difficulties in locating single fathers of all social classes. Thus, the search was terminated with the seventh custodial father. I did not attempt to interview noncustodial mothers at Time 1 because they were even more difficult to locate and I did not wish to extend the interviewing period further.

Apart from custodial fathers, a second focus of interest at Time 1 consisted in studying career women and comparing their life conditions with those of less privileged women. Consequently, of 26 women, 13 were of lower socioeconomic status (SES) and 13 of higher SES; of the 23 men, 9 were of lower SES and 14 were of higher SES.[1] The women's SES was their *own* at the time of interview and not that of their former spouse. The higher-SES persons were professionals, held managerial positions, owned businesses, one was a model, another a wealthy student, one a head nurse and two were high school teachers with a M.A. degree. Their yearly income averaged $33,000 and all had at least a B.A. In contrast, the lower-SES persons held skilled, semi-skilled and unskilled positions, all of the blue-collar category. Seven respondents were on welfare (two men and five women). Three skilled workers earned an average of $30,000 but the average income for the rest of the lower-SES respondents was $15,000. None of the lower-SES women earned more than $12,000 yearly. Not one person had advanced beyond high school. Therefore, we had succeeded in obtaining two contrasting sub-samples in terms of SES and life conditions.

The 49 respondents at Time 1 constituted a snowball sample: The referral technique had been used. The higher-SES group was initiated by one referral from a personal acquaintance while the lower-SES group was initiated in a government-subsidized high rise. However, the sample was not constituted by a chain of friends in that respondents were asked for names of persons they *knew of* rather than friends. For instance, a few employers who were among our interviewees referred employees and vice versa; other respondents gave addresses of persons in their previous neighborhood; a shop owner gave us the name of a client; schoolteachers referred pupils' parents; interviewed professionals gave us names of peers; women respondents gave us names of children's classmates whose parents were known to have separated. Consequently, respondents resided throughout the entire metropolitan Toronto area and were not located in one or two particular neighborhoods. Nor was the sample of clinical origins or biased by self-selection as only three of the initial referrals were not interviewed.

In the 27 single-parent families (20 headed by a woman and 7 by a man), the children's age ranged from three to eighteen, and the families had one to five children. Because observation of school-age children's behavior was part of the Time 1 design, no family was composed exclusively of preschoolers and all the children had to reside at the respondent's home. Custodial fathers' children were 12-years-old on the average and custodial mothers' children were 11. Custodial fathers had a lower average number of children than custodial mothers: 2 versus 2.9. Other studies have also found that men who have custody have older children than women with custody—probably because a man would find it more difficult to care for very young children, whereas, in our society, it is the role of women to do so. Although both groups of custodial mothers (low SES, high SES) had a comparable ratio of male to female children, custodial fathers had more male children: all custodial fathers had at least one son. Three even had no daughters—a large number considering that we had only seven custodial fathers. As other researchers have also found custodial fathers to have more sons than expected by chance (Grief 1985; Ferri 1976), it is suggested that the sex of the children, especially the presence of a male child, may be a motivating factor toward seeking custody on the part of fathers, and a contributing factor in a judge's decision to award custody where the father legally seeks it or contests it.

CUSTODIAL FATHERS AND MOTHERS

All but one of the seven custodial fathers had sought custody. In Mendes' terminology (1976), these fathers were "seekers." Excepting one father who was a millionaire, the yearly income of the custodial fathers averaged $50,000, well above the average for custodial mothers and even for the other divorced men in the sample. Therefore, fathers who had sought custody tended to have an above-average income, and tended to have sons more than daughters. In contrast, it is likely that fathers who are deserted (there was one such a case in the sample) or have to take custody for a variety of reasons beyond their control are more representative of divorced men in terms of finances and male/female ratio of children.

Pursuing Mendes' terminology, probably half of the custodial *mothers* were "assenters." That is, they had merely accepted custody as a fact. Several mothers pointed out that, while they had wanted a divorce, they had not wanted to become single parents. In fact, two women had not wanted custody but had been deserted before they could do anything about it. As the sample increased with the Times 2 and 3 waves, an increasing number of such reluctant custodial mothers was found. Research has, until now, largely overlooked the fact that many divorced mothers have custody but *do not want it*. However, because of social pressure placed on women concerning their maternal role (which is their "natural" role), it is unlikely that a researcher would be very successful at locating a sample of unwilling custodial mothers. Not too many women even want to admit it to themselves that they do not care to keep their children with them. The following is an illustration of one such a woman's dilemma expressed during an exchange with the researcher:

> From what you've been saying, I can see that you are having a difficult time with the children [she has five children and is on welfare].

> Ugh, well, ugh, I can't hide it, they're here, you can *see* that it's not easy [the children are in and out, constantly interrupting, ignoring what she tells them, and cussing at each other]. I wouldn't tell the social worker, she couldn't understand, she could cut me off if she thinks I am a bad mother, but I wish I didn't have my children. I just wish to God they had a decent father who could take them off my back. I just can't wait for them to grow up and leave me alone [starts sobbing].

> Why would the social worker think you're a bad mother? After all, your children *are* difficult and you seem to be doing your best [she actually tries very hard but she lives in a high-delinquency neighborhood].

> It's nice of you to say that, real nice. [Sighs.] What it boils down to is that if your children are rough, it's your fault. If on top of it all I tell them [case workers] I don't care for their type [the children's type], they will say it's all my fault, that if I cared more for them they would be good.

> Would they be?

> No. If they were nice children I *would* care for them more. It's not *my* fault if I don't care for them, they're mean to me.

> So you wouldn't tell anyone you don't want them.

> No, they would look down on me.

Two years later, when I returned for the follow-up interview, her teenage daughter had left for a premature marriage after becoming pregnant, and her oldest son was in jail. The interviewee was left with the less difficult children and was a happier mother and person.

TIME 2 SAMPLE: EX-SPOUSES

In 1981, or at Time 2, 48 of the 49 respondents were reinterviewed. (One man was reported by his ex-wife to have moved to Alberta.) In addition, the respondents' ex-spouses were also interviewed for a total of 98 respondents. Nine ex-spouses could not be located as they had moved away, but some of the initial respondents had divorced more than once and had a total of nine ex-spouses who could be interviewed. Consequently, at Time 2, not only was the sample size of separated/divorced respondents growing, but we had added a unique dimension in the literature on divorce: we had *sets of ex-spouses*. The dyadic perspective is one rarely used in the family literature.[2] Therefore, as White and Brinkerhoff point out, it is not surprising that few studies on divorce include both ex-spouses (e.g., Ahrons and Wallisch 1987; Goldsmith 1980). Interviewing two ex-spouses is even more difficult than interviewing a married couple.

Indeed, it was more difficult to locate the ex-spouses than to relocate the initial subjects. There were two reasons for this. First, some ex-spouses, as will be discussed in Chapter III, had not maintained contact and others had deserted so that they did not know each other's whereabouts and could not help locating the other ex-partner. Second, many, especially among the men, were resistant to the idea that I would talk to their ex-spouse, as is illustrated in the following exchange with a male respondent toward the end of his interview at Time 2.

> If I understand you correctly, you don't want me to interview her.

> Of course not! [Indignant] So that you'll tell her everything I told you! I am not stupid! [It had already been explained to him that confidentiality was assured, that no "tattletaling" would take place.]

> You don't have to worry about that, I am not going to tell her anything about you and I am not going to come back and tell you what she told me. I just can't do that. You see, if I did something like this, it would be unethical and I could be censored by my University. I wouldn't do it.

[Stroking his chin, thinking] Even so, you're a woman and you'll side with her. You'll believe everything she tells you. You'll compare our answers.

Yes, that is the purpose of this research: to see how ex-husbands and ex-wives agree and disagree. But that does not mean I will side with her. That's not my job. You know, there's always two sides to a coin and I am interested in finding out how this happens.

He relented and gave her address. One man refused, however; in his case, he had remarried *and* redivorced between the two interviews and I was seeking his *second* ex-wife. He had barely mentioned her during the interview. As both ex-wives told me, he had abandoned his second ex-wife in a rather shameful way. Fortunately, his oldest son was present and, as I was departing, he gave me the second wife's address: both son and mother had cared for the deserted second wife who had been abandoned while grievously ill and both felt very bad about her. She was interviewed in spite of the man's lack of cooperation. (It should be noted that he easily accepted being reinterviewed three years later.) These examples are only two illustrations of the difficulties inherent to interviewing ex-spouses. Other problems reside in moves out of the geographic area, for instance, and nine such cases had occurred by Time 2.

DESCRIPTION OF TIME 3 SAMPLE

In 1984, or at Time 3, 96 of the 98 respondents were reinterviewed while a questionnaire was given to their *new spouses* where applicable. When the new spouse had been divorced, his/her own ex-spouse was sought and interviewed while, once again, a questionnaire was given this person's new spouse where applicable. The focus of the Time 3 segment of the study, apart from its longitudinal aspects, was to study relationships between new spouses, between ex-spouses, and between one's new spouse and ex-spouse. The chains or networks of divorced and remarried persons consisted of 252 persons, as illustrated in the following diagram:

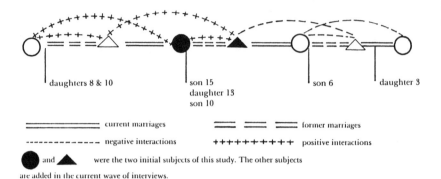

daughters 8 & 10   son 15   son 6   daughter 3
daughter 13
son 10

═════════ current marriages   ══ ══ ══ former marriages

------------- negative interactions   +++++++++ positive interactions

● and ▲ were the two initial subjects of this study. The other subjects
are added in the current wave of interviews.

The Time 3 sample, forms the basis of this book. Table II.1
presents the general characteristics of the 252 respondents.

The individuals described in Table II.1 included 95 ex-dyads
(two ex-spouses) as well as 103 remarriages, including 25 in which
a "new" child had been born. The sample contained 49 chains or
networks of divorced/remarried persons: each one of the initial
(Time 1) 49 respondents was at the origin of one chain.

THE MATTER OF SOCIAL CLASS

As indicated in Table II.1, SES was a key variable of this study.
Most studies on divorce/remarriage do not take this important
variable into consideration in their analysis. This lacuna is
especially detrimental in view of the fact that the sociological
literature contains hundreds and perhaps thousands of studies
which have documented the impact of SES on people's
opportunities and life circumstances. Apart from age and gender,
and in some societies, minority group status, social class is a key
determinant of an individual's life conditions. Therefore, it is
difficult to conceive that the experience of divorcing would not
be affected by this powerful social factor; yet, rare are the studies
on divorce which have controlled for SES.

It is entirely possible that some of the results of studies on divorce
are misleading and generalizations inappropriate because of this
lack of control for SES. For instance, suppose it is found that, after
divorce, people's overall happiness decreases by two points on a
5-point scale. This apparently substantial decrease may actually

Table II.1. Demographic Distribution of the Respondents in 1984

	Men								Women							
	Higher SES		Middle SES		Lower SES		Total		Higher SES		Middle SES		Lower SES		Total	
	(N)	%	(N)	%	(N)	%	(N)	%	(N)	%	(N)	%	(N)	%	(N)	%
Married	(3)	2.5	(8)	7.0	(0)	0.0	(11)	10.0	(11)	8.0	(10)	7.0	(2)	1.5	(23)	17.0
Living together	(0)	0.0	(2)	1.5	(2)	1.5	(4)	3.0	(0)	0.0	(1)	0.5	(1)	0.5	(2)	1.0
Remarried	(49)	42.0	(32)	27.0	(7)	6.0	(88)	75.0	(3)	22.0	(42)	31.0	(6)	4.0	(78)	58.0
Separated/divorced	(2)	1.5	(5)	4.0	(7)	6.0	(14)	12.0	(10)	7.0	(9)	7.0	(13)	10.0	(32)	24.0
Total	(54)	46%	(47)	40%	(16)	14%	(117)	100%	(51)	38%	(62)	46%	(22)	16%	(135)	100%

Average Age

	Men	Women
Married	33.5	28.0
Living Together	36.0	30.0
Remarried	40.5	35.9
Separated/divorced	40.9	41.2

13

camouflage the fact that higher-SES persons experience a decrease of only 0.5 whereas lower-SES persons experience one of over 2 points. Therefore, were this to occur, the experience of divorce would be highly qualified by one's social class membership and high status could be seen as a facilitator in the divorce process. When averaging is used and class is not controlled for, large class differences may become hidden. Indeed, in the dozens of statistical analyses performed on various parts of my data, SES was always a significant main effect, often more significant than gender and even marital status. Thus, SES is hardly a variable which we can afford to ignore. The problem becomes even more difficult when a sample of divorced persons is entirely middle class or, still, is below the poverty level. Generalizations concerning the entire experience of divorcing *have been* drawn from samples thusly skewed in terms of class or SES. It is no longer considered good sociology to use male samples and generalize to the entire population of a society, male *and* female. Similarly, a case can be made for the necessity to compare individuals from different classes before generalizing in the study of divorce, as in other studies.

INFORMATION GATHERING

The first phase of the study was, except for a few questions, entirely qualitative. The interviews were unstructured and totally open ended. A set of topics to be covered had been designed following ten pilot interviews. These selected topics could be covered in any order during the interviews. The respondents generally led the way and covered many of the topics without being prompted. Probes were added when necessary. Phase 1 was carried out in its earliest stage as an exploratory study. It is only in the later stages of interviewing (late 1979, early 1980) that the possibility of a follow-up study emerged.[3]

Time 2 (1981) interviews were structured and most questions were of the multiple-choice type. The respondents could, however, add anything they wanted and most offered lengthy comments on a variety of topics covered in the interviews. Many questions were retests of questions asked at Time 1 so as to cover the longitudinal aspect of the study. Above all else, Time 2 was designed as the groundwork for Time 3. Therefore, questions were added with the intent of retesting the respondents on these dimensions at a later date. Basically, the Time 2 phase was conceived as a follow-up to Phase 1 for the original subjects and as a stepping stone to Time 3 where a greater number of subjects would offer more quantitative longitudinal data than was possible with only 98 respondents. Because of the quantitative nature of North American sociology, I was keenly aware of the limitations in the size of the Time 1 and even Time 2 samples for publication purposes. Indeed, many of the journals to which I could submit articles were heavily statistical and demanded large, representative samples. However, a lack of resources precluded a sudden increase in the sample size itself during Time 2.

The Time 3 wave spanned the months of mid-February through October 1984 and involved a grant for computer programming as part of a sabbatical fellowship. Therefore, more sophisticated statistical analyses were possible. Time 3 represented different things for different respondents, depending on which phase of the research we had initially contacted them. For the 49 initial subjects, this was their third interview over a period of five and a half years on the average. For their 49 ex-spouses, first contacted in 1981, Time 3 represented their second interview. Indeed, Time 3 constitutes the longitudinal aspect of our study for 98 subjects or 48 ex-couples (and one ex-couple remarried to each other).

As indicated earlier, at Time 3, a substantial part of the interviews/questionnaires focused on the interrelationships in the networks, including the various children, stepchildren, the subjects' parents, parents-in-law, and ex-in-laws. In anthropological terms, the kinship relationships were studied, and included the affines as well as the ex-affines. For instance, I wanted to document what happens to one's relationship with one's affines after separation and remarriage, at which point one acquires new affines (Ambert 1988).

For Time 3, eleven overlapping but separate questionnaires had to be formulated in order to accommodate all possible types of individuals we might encounter. The individual focus of the eleven questionnaires is detailed in the notes.[4] The first four schedules detailed in footnote 4 had been designed for the 98 subjects already interviewed during the two previous phases. Schedules 5, 6, and 7 targeted the new spouses of these subjects as well as the new spouses of persons targeted in schedules 8 through 11. The latter schedules were intended for new spouses' ex-spouses. Actually, all persons targeted in schedules 5 through 11 fell under the rubric of "first interview." But the different labellings were needed to allow me to know where I was in a network as the series of interviews progressed.

Therefore, the 11 specific labels, although theoretically somewhat redundant in certain cases (for example, a person was labelled a new spouse or not a new spouse, even though he/she was a new spouse, depending on his or her placement in the network), were very useful during the fieldwork. If we mentally reproduce the diagram presented earlier and, above each person, add the schedule number used while interviewing that person, we see how the schedule labels allowed the author to retain a sense of where she was in a network while talking to a person. *Whose* ex-spouse was being interviewed? Indeed, avoiding blunders and potentially painful faux-pas was a constant concern in this research, as it was very difficult to keep in mind *who* was being interviewed in relation to the others who had already been interviewed or were to be interviewed in each network. The situation was especially complicated when a network contained one or two persons who had been divorced several times. As the number of ex-spouses multiplied, so did their own new spouses, and the latter's own ex-spouses with their new spouses. This disorientation problem will become evident in Chapters V and VIII. In addition to the 11 schedules, code numbers were designed for each category of respondents, again to help the researcher maintain her sense of direction and also to prepare for computer programming. Particularly complex was the task of pairing ex-spouses and even new spouses.

RESPONDENT COOPERATION

Few persons refused to participate in the study and, of those who accepted, few did so reluctantly. For instance, only 2% of the total respondents were judged to be uncooperative during the interviews. This high success rate, in spite of the longitudinal aspect from 1978 through 1984, and in spite of the highly sensitive nature of the interview, can probably be attributed to the perceived social status of the researcher. The fact that the researcher was a

"Dr." and a faculty member at one of the two universities in Toronto lent legitimacy to her request as well as an aura of responsibility, confidentiality, and clinical competence that a hired interviewer could not attain. It was possible to gain entry into the homes of the rich as well as of the poor. The rich liked conversing with a professor and did not feel diminished socially by the encounter as they might have if an assistant or a student had been sent to them.

As for the less fortunate, the titles helped because they perceived the researcher as a source of information. When advice was sought by the respondents, it was given if the topic fell within my areas of competence; otherwise, a few referrals were suggested. In other instances, when a respondent or a child in the home was obviously physically ill or malnourished but did not perceive it, steps were suggested to begin to remedy the situation. Fortunately, such drastic measures were rarely needed and because the sample included such a disproportionate number of educated and financially comfortable persons, I did not have to intervene frequently in the lives of the individuals. However, I consider the interviews themselves to be a form of intervention or intrusion, depending on one's perspective.

The sample is not random but is a stratified convenience sample, as described earlier. Therefore, it is not the purpose of this study to offer generalizations concerning divorce and remarriage in general in Canada and the United States. This study was designed to offer hypotheses and ideas, and present theories which could be tested on larger and, especially, more representative samples. This is an idea-generating study. However, given the care taken to have as diverse a sample as possible within the SES, parental status, and gender categories initially selected, this sample provides possibilities for *generalizing to groups similar to those represented in the sample.*

Indeed, although a few studies of divorce and remarriage claim to have random samples, the proportion located and interviewed from the sample initially targeted is often low—at times represents a mere one-third of the potential respondents. Others have a higher response rate but are based on court records, therefore excluding persons who initially separate out of court. Although the researchers generally present statistics indicating little difference in the age or age at divorce or number of years married between the subjects and those persons in the original pool, these variables are too demographic and too vague for a claim of randomness. If people cannot be located or refuse to be interviewed, this in itself indicates a source of potential differences. *The sample herein had very few refusals and lost very few persons over time. It is perhaps no less representative, within its range of selected demographic characteristics, than samples in studies claiming random samples but with high rates of refusal and failure to locate.*

RESEARCHER OBSERVATIONS

In this section, we will briefly discuss a current trend in the sociology of the family, including the field of divorce and remarriage. More and more studies in this field are carried out on the basis of large random samples drawn for public surveys by government agencies or for research purposes. In many cases, the authors who write reports have not been involved in the design, have not done a single interview, and can only proceed via statistical analyses of data not gathered to be analyzed in a particular way.

This trend derives in part from the infatuation with statistics and large representative samples which North American sociologists labor under. The gatekeepers of the best journals (the referees and the editors) feel uncomfortable with qualitative material and smallish samples. They become overly concerned with a few key points: representativeness of sample and statistics. It does not seem to occur to them that certain topics cannot be studied in depth via statistics. Indeed, statistics present results but rarely *explain* the *processes* which have led to the results. Only qualitative and observational material can explain processes in depth. Thus, we are accumulating *results* but possess few clues as to how these have occurred. Neither do journal referees show much inclination to accept articles which illustrate how new questions should be studied when the sample is "small," or "nonrandom."

Although there is a great deal of merit in doing large-scale surveys, it is questionable whether researchers who have never met *any* of the respondents interviewed have a clear understanding of what is going on. The best approach would be for researchers to *participate* in large-scale surveys, especially at the interview level, and to gather *qualitative material* that would give them more insight into the various results. It is not only a question of fleshing out the results but of understanding their sources and processes.

With the current trend, we may be heading toward the development of an armchair sociology: groups of sociologists who have never met any of their survey's respondents. The statistics do not give any idea of the body language that can be read during a face-to-face interview. Signals of doubt, anger, pride, depression, deceit, happiness go unreported that could make a great deal of difference. The respondent's typical appearance is ignored: it is not seen. But does it not mean something that a respondent is emaciated, dirty, or is obese and perhaps too well manicured? And what about the respondent's style of interaction during the interview? The following is taken from notes made in the car five minutes after an interview had been completed at Time 1. During the interview, the respondent had expressed a desire to remarry soon and have a baby (he had three teenagers who lived with their mother).

> He received me with a large, babyish smile. He was fidgety, joked constantly, and evaded about a dozen questions. He discussed everything under the sun and is very sophisticated. Seemed very self-centered and selfish when discussing his ex-spouse. Told me he wanted to remarry soon and have a baby. When I was about to leave, the screen door got stuck. He joked about it and I handed him the baby [researcher's 9-month-old daughter] to fix the door. He held her at arms' length, rigidly, not knowing what to do, rather terrified by the situation. I wondered how can he want a baby and what did he do when the others were small? He is the only male respondent with children who didn't pick her up during an interview.

This professional man, relatively well-to-do, was indeed to remarry a few months after this interview and redivorce six months later when his young bride became ill with an acute case of arthritis. He explained, in the second interview, that he had been "a good catch" for her and that she had deceived him by becoming ill: "I didn't get remarried to become a nurse." He was the one respondent described earlier who had refused to help locate that second wife. That he wanted to remarry to have a child was interesting datum. However, this datum acquired an entirely new dimension when placed within the context of the above vignette, and in comparison to the behavior exhibited by other men. (Behavior is not reported in surveys: only answers are.)

He had described his first ex-wife as a real battle axe and I was not actually looking forward to interviewing *her*. However, she materialized to be a sophisticated, warm, direct and honest respondent who never evaded a question although she was not overly talkative. She was not reticent but reserved. She interacted easily and firmly with their children. The children had happened to be at his home during his second interview: *all* his interactions with them were at the joking level. One had a sense of his being "tacked on" his family rather than belonging to it. Again, this observation of behavior added a great deal of counterweight to this respondent's interview schedule.

The observations made by any researcher may be one of the most revealing research methods employed in the field of family studies. Yet, we are leaving behind this more "anthropological" approach, and depriving our studies on human beings of their humaneness. By their physical appearance, their body language, their style of interaction, respondents reveal as much, and sometimes more, than in the close-ended questions. It is difficult to maintain a constant facade of "social desirability" during a 3-hour interview with a trained researcher. The researcher is more likely to obtain the "truth" by mixing research techniques: observations, verbatim quotes, and "hard" data.

Another example will illustrate the advantages of in-depth interviews within a naturalistic setting. One welfare mother of five children was entirely bruised facially and a tooth was missing. One eye was blackened and puffy. Even her arms had large, blue and brown spots. She was at first very uncomfortable but began to relax after one hour. Her children were in and out: two appeared mentally deficient or slow and she confirmed that they were in Special Education classes. After two hours, I broached the topic of her physical appearance by saying, "Now, don't tell me you fell down the stairs." She had probably rehearsed the answer and she confessed that she had just broken up with a man who had beaten her up. The explanation was plausible, especially so since she had already described how her ex-husband used to assault her physically.

A little later in the four-hour interview, her 16-year-old son (oldest child) came in the kitchen: immediately, I sensed that something was wrong. She became tense, agitated, and kept looking at her son apprehensively. While pretending to wash his hands, he examined me sideways and suspiciously. I introduced myself and the topic of my study. He shrugged and walked out slamming the door. We looked at each other: she was shaking and ashen.

> Do you care to talk about him? I can see you are afraid of him. It is O.K., you can tell me, I won't tell anyone.

> [Silence]

> Well, alright, we'll talk about something else. But you know, it might just make you feel better to tell me about it. Does he rough you up?

> [Sobs]

And she talked. For the first time since this had begun. Not only was the experience cathartic, but the face-to-face encounters in her home setting provided more valuable information than all the questionnaire items did. The role of the sociologist can be enhanced with the addition of an ethnographic dimension. Presentation of such data should be encouraged, rather than discouraged by the sociology establishment.

NOTES

1.   Socioeconomic status (or SES) was determined using the 1976 revision of the Blishen scale which is adapted to the Canadian classification of occupations, related income, education, and prestige. Blishen and Roberts (1976) suggest class intervals of ten digits from the scores received by each occupation. We have followed this rule with two modifications in order to meet the SES distinctions found in our sample as well as to take into consideration socioeconomic changes which have occurred since 1976 in Metropolitan Toronto. Thus, our sample was subdivided into seven strata: the lower-lower SES (scores of 30-), upper-lower SES (30-39), lower-middle SES (40-49), middle-middle SES (50-59), upper-middle SES (60+) and a lower-upper SES which includes certain categories from the previous level but commanding higher prestige and income. It should be noted that we had contemplated a higher-upper SES segment of society's leaders but no individual in this survey fell within this theoretical bracket.

Women's SES was determined strictly on the basis of their own occupation when gainfully employed or even doing full-time unpaid volunteer work. Thus, most women's SES is achieved and not derived from that of their spouses, current or past. Homemakers neither gainfully employed nor filling a volunteer slot received their current husband's SES if their own educational level and last occupation were the equivalent to that of their spouse. Those women with a lower level of such were placed on the lower adjacent SES stratum. The few homemakers still unremarried who were unemployed were on welfare and were placed in the lower SES stratum.

2. For references, please consult next chapter.

3. Three reports were written based on the results of the Time 1 wave. One focused on differences in children's behavior toward custodial mothers and custodial fathers (Ambert 1982a). Another studied the medical drug use of the respondents (Ambert 1982b), while a third focused on the remarriage expectations and tactics of the women (Ambert 1983).

4. 1. Persons separated/divorced once, already interviewed, remarried;
    2. Persons separated/divorced once, already interviewed, unremarried;
    3. Persons separated/divorced more than once, already interviewed, remarried;
    4. Persons separated/divorced more than once, already interviewed, unremarried;
    5. New spouses of formerly divorced persons: first marriage;
    6. New spouses of formerly divorced persons: remarriage (previously divorced or widowed);
    7. New spouses of formerly divorced persons: remarriage (divorced more than once);
    8. Persons separated/divorced once, first interview, remarried;
    9. Persons separated/divorced once, first interview, unremarried;
    10. Persons separated/divorced more than once, first interview, remarried;
    11. Persons separated/divorced more than once, first interview, unremarried.

Chapter III

Relationship Between Ex-Spouses

Surely, you do not expect me to tell you that I see my ex-wife every other day! [Laughs.] If you have and ex-wife it's because you don't want to see her!

—Man, business owner

My ex-husband? We get along better now than we used to while married. I think it is because we are now both independent of each other. We are parents but this does not mean we have to be tied down to each other. It took us a while to understand this.

—Woman, business career

Sometimes I think I should have stayed ... but if I had stayed he probably would not have bothered to improve himself. I bet he started making money just to teach me a lesson. I hate him.

—Woman, clerical worker

So, no, I don't know exactly where she is but last year I heard she had gotten another poor sucker to fall for her. This woman is bad news. I wasted six years of my life on her.

—Man, skilled worker

Over one million divorces take place annually in North America. Thus, each year, over two million persons become ex-spouses. In spite of the commonplace of this phenomenon, researchers are only beginning to map the contours of the ex-spousal relationship (Wallerstein and Kelly 1980) without actually knowing several of its intricacies. Perhaps one reason for this gap in the literature is that a *study of the relationship between ex-spouses would require that both ex-spouses be interviewed.* But few studies of intact marriages include both spouses (Ahrons and Bowman 1981; Ball et al. 1983; Safilios-Rothschild 1969; Szinovacz 1983), and even when they do the dyadic approach is frequently not explored. Therefore, as White and Brinkerhoff (1978) point out, it is not surprising that few studies of divorce include both ex-spouses.

Researchers have already discussed the fact that there are no institutionalized norms concerning this relationship (Burgoyne and Clark 1984; Goode 1956). However, researchers and clinicians generally agree that it is important for ex-spouses to cooperate as parents (Ahrons 1979, 1980; Rosenthal and Keshet 1981), but that those persons who are unable to relinquish their attachment to the ex-spouse or who maintain too frequent contact with him/her do not adjust to divorce as smoothly (Kurdek and Blisk 1983; Rosenthal and Keshet 1981; Spanier and Thompson 1984). Many studies show that divorced partners maintain at least a mild attachment (Brown et al. 1980; Goldsmith 1980; Kitson 1982; Spanier and Thompson 1984), and Price-Bonham and Balswick (1980) have even qualified divorce "as an incident in the relationship of spouses rather than an ending." However, Furstenberg points to a "ritual avoidance" which takes place when there are no children (see also, Albrecht 1980). In addition, a great deal of hostility often remains after divorce (Furstenberg 1982; Hetherington, Cox, and Cox 1979, 1982) with the children and finances serving as the vehicles for the ventilation of this hostility (Hetherington et al. 1982; Richards 1982).

Studies also indicate that the adjustment of the custodial parent is greatly facilitated when a supportive coparental relationship exists (Hetherington et al. 1982; Kurdek and Blisk 1983; Nelson 1981; Rosenthal and Keshet 1981; Wallerstein and Kelly 1980). Moreover, research shows that the presence of children from the previous marriage constitutes the main link between the ex-spouses (Ahrons and Wallisch 1986; Bloom and Kindle 1985; Clingempeel 1981; Goetting 1979; Kurdek and Blisk 1983; Luepnitz 1982; Rosenthal and Keshet 1981). Nevertheless, there are also indications that a substantial proportion of noncustodial parents rarely, if at all, see their children (Eekelaar and Clive 1977; Furstenberg and Spanier 1984), and this distancing increases over time (Furstenberg and Nord 1985; Murch 1980; Seltzer and Bianchi

1988), although we have no information on what takes place after these children have become adults. Once adults, how do children of divorce relate to the parent they have rarely seen?

This chapter will explore (1) the norms that divorced and remarried persons hold concerning their relationship with an ex-spouse, and (2) how they evaluate their own performance and that of their ex-spouse in light of these norms. Next, the frequency of contacts between the ex-spouses and the help they provide each other is assessed at the behavioral level. Then it will be determined if the presence of children from their previous marriage has any effect on their relationship; the effect of gender and socioeconomic status will also be studied as well as that of remarriage. How ex-spouses evaluate each other as parents when they share children: Do they feel their ex-wife or ex-husband is a good parent? Again, some variables will be discussed that could affect this evaluation, such as socioeconomic status and, especially, parental status. That is, are custodial parents more or less satisfied with the ex-spouse than noncustodial parents? In view of the fact that at least one-third of the noncustodial parents rarely, if ever, see their children and that only one-third of noncustodial fathers pay child support on a regular basis, it could be reasonable to expect a great deal of dissatisfaction on the part of the parents who have child custody.

This chapter will then look into the *feelings* ex-spouses have for each other as well as their perception of each other's feelings. How accurate are ex-husbands and ex-wives in assessing the other's feelings for self? This will be pursued by going one step beyond and look at actual feelings *within dyads*: Do ex-spouses have the same feelings for each other or do they tend to hold different feelings? In terms of their *relationship*, do ex-spouses evaluate it similarly or differently?

How do ex-dyads who hold similar feelings and evaluate their relationship similarly differ from ex-dyads in which both ex-spouses feel differently about each other? What characterizes an ex-couple friendly for each other as compared to an embattled one?

NORMATIVE RELATIONSHIP

Toward the very end of the Time 3 interviews, I asked respondents the following questions:[1]

I'll ask your opinion on something to which you must have given much thought. How should ex-husbands and wives behave toward each other?

- should they treat each other courteously?   yes ... no ...
- should they talk against each other?   yes ... no ...
- should they keep to themselves what went on in
  private between them?   no ... yes ...
- should they treat each other with love?   yes ... no ...
- should they be friends ... or just neutral ... or distant ...?   ·
- should they stand by each other if they share children?   yes ... no ...

Then, respondents were asked to evaluate their own behavior vis-à-vis the ex-spouse as well as the ex-spouse's behavior toward them: "I treat my ex-wife the way I think it should be" or "I do not treat her the way I think it should be" or "I do not have anything to do with her."

A very high consensus emerged among the respondents on four of the six normative indicators concerning the proper way of conducting a post-marital relationship: ex-spouses should treat each other courteously (92%), should not talk against each other (98%), should not treat each other with love (98%), and should stand by each other when they share children (97%). On the matter of keeping to themselves what had happened between them, 73% of the respondents agreed that this should be the norm. However, they were quite divided as to the form of their actual relationship: 28% responded that they should be friends, while 34% felt that they should remain distant, and 37% believed that they should be neutral. In view of the high consensus expressed, no significant differences emerged by gender and SES, although higher-SES respondents tended to be more inclined toward friendliness and the more polite forms of relationship. Later, it will be shown how these small normative differences by SES might be reflected in behavior.

How did respondents feel they were treating their ex-spouse and were treated by him or her in light of their expressed normative preferences? Fifty-nine percent of the respondents believed that they treated their ex-spouse correctly, while 41% believed that their ex-spouse treated *them* correctly. Women tended to feel that they treated their ex-husband less well than should be the case, while ex-husbands believed that they treated their ex-wife very well indeed. In addition, women felt that they were not as well treated as should be the case by their ex-husband, while fewer ex-husbands felt that their ex-wife was not treating them properly. Thus, overall, women more readily admitted than men not treating their ex-spouse according to normative expectations and also felt not so well treated in return—although none of the differences was near significance level. Therefore, it can be said that women's normative expectations on how to conduct an ex-spousal relationship were not as fulfilled as those of men. Women were more dissatisfied than men in this respect, just as studies on marriage find that women are less satisfied maritally than men. There seems to be some continuity of gender difference in the fulfillment of one's expectations between marriage and the post-marital period.

FREQUENCY OF CONTACTS

Four questions measured contacts: two were general and two were specific in terms of time. The respondents were asked: "How often do you talk to your ex-wife [ex-husband] over the phone?" They were also asked how often they generally visited with their ex-spouse. In both instances, the multiple choices and the coding were as follows:

alternatives	coded as
once a week or more every other week once a month	often
every other month 3-4 times a year	irregularly
once a year rarely never	rarely

At a more immediate level, the interviewees were asked if they had talked with their ex-spouse over the phone in the past *week* (yes or no), and if they had visited with the ex-spouse during the past *month* (yes or no). For visits, the past *month* was used instead of the past week as had been the case for telephone contacts: pretests had indicated that recall of phone contacts was not accurate past one week; however, recall of visits was longer. Moreover, because visits were infrequent, a one-month period allowed for a greater frequency of visits than a one-week period would have, thus facilitating statistical analysis.

A prior analysis of the couple data indicated that ex-husbands and ex-wives within each ex-dyad agreed in over 92% of the cases on how often they visited with each other and talked to each other. Thus, since the men in this sample generally were the ex-husbands of the women, only women's answers were analyzed for frequency of contacts. We chose to use women rather than men for the simple reason that women were slightly more numerous than men and thus offered an overview on a greater number of ex-couples.

In terms of contacts *in general,* 83% of the nonparents visited with their ex-spouse only rarely, if at all (Table III.1). However, when they shared children, ex-spouses saw each other frequently in 44% of the cases, irregularly in another 23%, and rarely in 34% of the cases. Although the presence of children from the previous marriage contributed to a greater frequency of contacts between ex-spouses, it is still noteworthy that one-third of the parents rarely, if ever, saw each other. Moreover, when considering SES, we see in Table III.1 that 41% of the lower-SES women reported rarely visiting with their children's father while only 28% of the higher-SES women reported the same. One half of the higher-SES mothers (51%) frequently saw their ex-spouse, but 34% of the lower-SES mothers did. This SES difference can be explained in part by the greater proportion of ex-husbands who had deserted at the lower-SES level rather than by the age of the children. Children's age was uniform across SES levels.

The phone contacts in general were also more frequent when there were children (Table III.2): while 44% of parents were in frequent phone contact, only two sets of ex-spouses (or 7.7%) who did not have children were. Moreover, as indicated in Table III.2, the frequency of phone contacts was significantly affected among parents by the mothers' SES, not so much at the "frequently" level as at the "rarely" level where only 13% of the higher-SES mothers reported themselves to be in contrast to 41% of the lower-SES mothers.

Turning to *recent* contacts between the ex-spouses (not presented in tabular form), only the presence of children created a difference: overall, one-third of the mothers had talked to their ex-husband in the past week while only three childless women (or

Table III.1. Frequency of Women's Visits with Ex-Husbands
by SES and Presence of Children from Previous Marriage

| Frequency of Visits | Higher SES* | | | | Lower SES** | | | |
| | Children | | No Children | | Children | | No Children | |
	(N)	%	(N)	%	(N)	%	(N)	%
Frequently	(20)	51	(2)	8	(11)	34	(1)	10
Irregularly	(8)	21	(2)	8	(8)	25	(1)	10
Rarely	(11)	28	(22)	85	(13)	41	(8)	80
Totals	(39)		(26)		(32)		(10)	

Notes: No significant difference between SES, either with children or childless.
    * $p < .001$; chi-square $= 20.20201$, 2 df.
    ** $p < .0932$; chi-square $= 4.74687$, 2 df.

8.6%) had done so. Visiting with the ex-spouse was a rare occurrence as only 15% of the women had done so in the past month: higher-SES mothers visited with their ex-spouse more often than higher-SES childless women (38% versus 25%), and even more often than lower-SES mothers (18.8%). These results were corroborated by the ex-husbands.

In certain respects up to this point, behavior followed norms while in other respects it lagged behind norms expressed by the respondents in terms of coparenting: not only had parents more contacts than childless ex-spouses, but a comparison of each parent's stated norm with stated behavior indicated that the four parents who had responded that parents should *not* stand by each other were fathers who never saw their children or their children's mother. Nevertheless, behavior lagged behind expressed norms among a majority of the men who never or rarely saw their children's mother and opted for a norm of coparental responsibility. In terms of SES we had seen that the higher-SES respondents tended toward friendlier norms and, in reality, their contacts were also more frequent.

After so many years of separation, there were only two sets of ex- spouses in which one still helped the other on practical matters such as car maintenance. However, the earlier data (1981 or Time 2) on the 98 longitudinal subjects clearly indicated a higher frequency, not only of contacts, but of help two years after separation, especially when children were involved. This is in

Table III.2.   Frequency of Women's Phone Contact with Ex-Husbands by SES and Presence of Children from Previous Marriage

	Higher SES*				Lower SES**			
	Children***		No Children		Children***		No Children	
Frequency of Visits	(N)	%	(N)	%	(N)	%	(N)	%
Frequently	(18)	46	(2)	7.7	(13)	41	(0)	0
Irregularly	(16)	.41	(2)	7.7	(6)	19	(0)	0
Rarely	(5)	13	(22)	85.0	(13)	41	(10)	100
Totals	(39)		(26)		(32)		(10)	

Notes: * $p < .001$; chi-square = 33.11728, 2 df.
          ** $p < .0004$; chi-square = 10.84239, 2 df.
          *** $p < .0158$; chi-square = 8.29798, 2 df between higher and lower SES with children.

accordance with the results of Spanier and Thompson (1984) whose respondents, separated an average of only two years, had far more frequent contacts (and ambivalent relationships) than our respondents who, by Time 3, had been separated for six years. Thus, both the longitudinal and the cross-studies data indicate a withering of contacts between ex-spouses over time.

QUALITY OF THE RELATIONSHIP

Analysis of the qualitative data indicated that respondents differentiated between visiting with (our indicator) and seeing the ex-spouse from a distance or for a few minutes when they picked up or left their children at the other spouse's home, or when they inadvertently ran into each other at an adult child's home. Planned visits were usually avoided (Furstenberg's "mutual avoidance") and were deemed necessary only for the children's sake: "If we didn't have children there'd be no need to see her. I'd prefer it this way. An ex-wife is a relationship you prefer not to maintain, otherwise why divorce?" A feeling of being burdened by the past marital relationship because of the children was frequently articulated. Respondents expressed a desire to "wipe the slate clean" and forget entirely about their ex-spouse, but felt they were not in a position to do so because of the children.

It is not that I do not like him or have any resentment but I would like to make a clean cut and I simply cannot do that because of the children. He really is the only person I feel I can bother about their problems. I don't want to bore my friends with them, and this means seeing him much more than I thought I would have to at the age our children have reached. But I need to talk to someone about them.

I don't have anything against her but I simply don't care to see her. She is not my wife any more. It's very difficult to want to be truly divorced from someone and have nothing to do with them, yet having to see her on a regular basis because of the children. In other words, it is impossible to wipe the slate clean with children.

There were six respondents, however, who were pleased to have the children as an excuse to maintain a relationship with their ex-spouse or who felt this to be the case with the ex-spouse: "I phone him. I guess I lean on him, as I always have ... If I didn't have the children? Well, I guess it would be hard for me to lean on him as I would have no reason to do so. I see what you're getting at, the children provide me with an excuse and that's true."

Respondents were asked to evaluate the quality of their relationship and were given the following choices: generally warm and friendly; sometimes friendly; cordial; distant; usually unfriendly; no relationship. In Table III.3, the ex-wives' answers are presented vertically while the ex-husbands' answers are presented horizontally. This grid pattern indicates that 17 of the 85 ex-dyads (or 20%) for whom we were able to gather the relevant information were congruent in terms of having a generally friendly relationship. In other words, in 20% of the ex-dyads both ex-spouses agreed that their relationship was very good. Another 20% agreed that it was very bad ("usually unfriendly") and 27% agreed that no relationship existed. In all 78.8% of the ex-dyads consisted of two ex-spouses who agreed on the quality of their relationship, whether good, bad, or nonexistent. We also note in Table III.3 that, when there was disagreement, it was generally minor rather than radical.

In order to evaluate further the type of relationship respondents had with their ex-spouse we asked them what they talked about with each other. The answer always had something to do with the children:

Table III.3. Ex-Wives' and Ex-Husbands' Evaluation of Their Relationship with Each Other

Ex-Husbands' Evaluation	Ex-Wives' Evaluation													
	Friendly		Sometimes Friendly		Cordial		Distant		Usually Unfriendly		No Relationship		Row Totals	
	(N)	%	(N)	%	(N)	%	(N)	%	(N)	%	(N)	%	(N)	%
Friendly	(17)	89.5* / 85.0** / 20.0***	(2)	10.5 / 16.7 / 2.4									(19)	22.4%
Sometimes friendly	(3)	27.3 / 15.0 / 3.5	(7)	63.6 / 58.3 / 8.2	(1)	9.1 / 100.0 / 1.2							(11)	12.9%
Cordial							(1)	100.0 / 14.3 / 1.2					(1)	1.2%
Distant							(3)	60.0 / 42.9 / 3.5	(2)	40.0 / 9.1 / 2.4			(5)	5.9%
Usually unfriendly			(3)	13.6 / 25.0 / 3.5			(2)	9.1 / 28.6 / 2.4	(17)	77.3 / 77.3 / 20.0			(22)	25.9%
No relationship							(1)	3.7 / 14.3 / 1.2	(3)	11.1 / 13.6 / 3.5	(23)	85.2 / 100.0 / 27.1	(27)	31.8%
Column totals														
(N)	(20)		(12)		(1)		(7)		(22)		(23)		(85)	
%		23.5%		14.1%		1.2%		8.2%		25.9%		27.1%		100.0%

Notes: * Ex-Husbands' percentage. ** Ex-Wives' percentage. *** Total percentage.

32

Mainly about wedding arrangements, gifts for the children and grandchildren, surprise parties.

Always about a conflict in the children's visiting schedule. I don't even bother anymore asking him for money. I have never brought up his remarriage although he has tried to insinuate it in the conversation but I cut him short because I know he wants to brag and why should I be the target?

Respondents stressed the importance of avoiding personal topics such as dating, remarriage, and even feelings for each other. There was a great deal of unanimity in this respect, once more an indication that at least covert norms exist concerning the ex-spousal relationship. However, interestingly enough, twelve respondents indicated that they had felt less constrained to remain within these boundaries of "taboo" subjects after *both* had remarried. At that point, many would routinely inquire about the new spouse's health, work, likings, for instance. A few rare respondents had somewhat more general conversations and expressed an interest in each other's opinion and life. But again, these involved instances where both ex-spouses had remarried, as in the following quote:

We catch up on all the news like old friends. Some of our friends have even forgotten we were ever married ..... He calls me on my birthdays. We talk about our work mainly. On that front we had a lot in common, too much for a marriage [laughs] but it fits nicely into a post-marital format .... I wouldn't mind seeing more of him but I am happy also as things stand. He is like a brother to me now and vice versa I am certain. Nothing is left, not even bitterness.

THE EX-SPOUSE AS SOURCE OF HELP

In another section of the interview, respondents were given a list of 18 categories of persons and asked to check those persons whom they turn to most often for help. They could check as many persons as deemed necessary, and the ex-spouse was included in the list. Then, from the same list, they had to choose *three* persons whom they considered *most* helpful to them. Answers were coded as yes or no concerning each person in the list.

As will be shown, few respondents chose the ex-spouse. This skewed response distribution at the "no" level meant that we could not analyze the data within a dyadic perspective. Both men and women were included in the analysis because there was no automatic agreement between ex-spouses on this dimension: indeed, one ex-spouse can be more useful to the other, whether because of resources, personal attributes, or family situation.

Only 16% of the respondents chose their first ex-spouse as a person they turned to most often for help. (Not one of the 19 multiply-divorced mentioned a second or third ex-spouse in this area.) Thus, the ex-spouse was ranked eleventh of 18 possibilities, with the current spouse coming first (62.5%), followed by parents (39%) and sisters (37%). When asked to choose the three persons who were the most helpful, 12% of the respondents chose the first ex-spouse in comparison to 52.6% for the current spouse. Therefore, overall, the ex-spouse was considered to be an infrequent source of help for most persons and was not salient in the life of the other as a most helpful person.

When there were no children, men never mentioned their ex-wife as a person they turned to for help but three higher-SES women did. When there were children, 25% of the women and 16% of the men turned to their ex-spouse for help, and higher-SES parents did so more often than lower-SES parents, specially among women. Thus, one-third of higher-SES mothers counted their ex-husband as a main source of help. Eight of the eleven fathers who turned to their ex-wife for help were of higher SES. These figures, and those in the previous section, imply that there is a greater coparental cohesiveness among higher-SES than lower-SES persons. Or, put otherwise, after separating, higher-SES persons were better equipped to play their coparental roles than were lower-SES persons.

The type of help ex-spouses gave each other generally focused on the children babysitting, help in disciplining, advice, school activities. Being able to talk to the other ex-spouse about problems created by the children was often mentioned as a form of help rather than as something taken for granted. There were six ex-couples who even helped each other with the children from their remarriage.

Table III.4. Repondents' Evaluation of the Ex-Spouse As a Parent[a]

Gender[b]				SES[c]						Custodial Status[d]					
Men		Women		Higher		Middle		Lower		Custodial		Noncustodial		Children on Their Own	
X̄	(N)	X̄	(N)	X̄	(N)	X̄	(N)	X̄	(N)	X̄	(N)	X̄	(N)	X̄	(N)
1.9	(71)	2.58	(81)	2.3	(63)	2.0	(62)	3.0	(27)	2.6	(57)	1.7	(56)	2.2	(18)

Notes: [a] 1 = very good; 5 = very bad.
[b] t test, F = 1.63, 150 df., p < .001.
[c] chi-square = 19.255, 8 df., p < .0136.
[d] chi-square = 17.26786, 8 df., p < .0276.

PERCEPTION OF THE EX-SPOUSE AS A PARENT

"All in all, how good a parent is your ex-wife [ex-husband]?" The alternatives were very good, good, could be better, and could be much better." To these was added a fifth choice; "terrible," by six women respondents. In Table III.4, we see that women rated their ex-husbands much less favorably as a parent than did men. Not only did six women believe that their former husband was a "terrible" father but, of the 30 respondents who chose the next to worst choice of "could be much better," 22 were also women. This gender difference remained when comparing social classes: both men and women in the lowest SES gave a less favorable rating to their ex-spouse than persons in the other classes. This latter finding is tied to the fact that lower-SES ex-spouses saw each other less frequently and rarely coparented, in great part due to the desertion of fathers and lack of support of mothers.

As anticipated, we see in Table III.4 that noncustodial parents provided the best rating when compared to custodial parents and parents whose children were living on their own. There were 19 custodial parents (18 of whom were custodial mothers) who described their ex-spouse as either a terrible parent or one who could be much better. Custodial fathers rated their ex-spouse more favorably than custodial mothers, in great part because, in this sample, all but one noncustodial mother kept in close touch with their children. In contrast, one-third of the noncustodial fathers rarely, if at all, saw their children, and many more did not contribute to their support (see Arendell 1986).

Even within ex-dyads, fathers rated mothers more highly than mothers rated fathers, with the exception of friendly dyads in which each ex-spouse held the other in high esteem. Because mothers were definitely closer to their children than fathers (probably in great part because of custody arrangements) and were doing much more for them than fathers it is logical that mothers were judged to be better parents. They actually were. What follows is a sample of comments made by ex-spouses on each other as parents.

> He would be very good if he were supportive of my children's relationship with me. He thinks he is doing what is best for them but he is doing what is best for *him*.

He is a good man but he is a poor example [to the children]. I often have to tell him how to behave with them such as not to praise them when the report cards are terrible and not to scold them when they're good. He's just too inconsistent.

She tries to be very good and I think she is very devoted but her lifestyle could have such a damaging impact on the children's future that she can't be considered an excellent parent. However, she does take an excellent care of the children and I never worry about it.

The poor example set by the other parent, generally the noncustodial, is a recurrent theme: " ... he also gives such a bad example out of his own life. What do you think a boy can learn from a father ... who abuses drugs himself, has a series of wives, can't stop talking about sex?"

Some of the respondents talked about their own role in helping their children appreciate the other parent. Again, such comments were generally made by mothers, but fathers also made them: "I think they have more fun living with me than with her but I have raised them to love their mother; it's very important in their development and I've found that *I* am a better man for it."

FEELINGS TOWARD EX-SPOUSE: THE INDIVIDUAL PERSPECTIVE

Respondents were asked how they currently felt about their ex-spouse. This question focused specifically on personal *feelings* while a previous question presented in Table III.3 had focused on the quality of the *relationship*. The alternatives were: "I am still in love"; "I am not in love but I miss him/her very much"; "Friendly but I don't miss him/her"; "Just as happy if I don't see him/her"; "Actually dislike him/her"; "Angry at him/her"; "Indifference." Later on, they were asked, "How would you describe your ex-husband's [ex-wife's] feelings for you now?" The same categories as above were used with the addition of "I don't know."

The results (not presented in tabular form) certainly did not support any continued or deep attachment to the ex-spouse after an average of 6.2 years of separation, and, for those remarried, an average of two years of remarriage: only one man and five women missed the ex-spouse. There were no significant gender differences in type of feelings expressed. Among men, there were no SES differences. However, among women, higher-SES women tended to feel indifferent far more than lower-SES women (40% vs. 19%), while lower-SES women tended to be angrier and disliked their ex-spouse more than higher-SES women (36% vs. 15%). This class difference among women was related to the greater difficulties that the divorce had plunged lower-SES women into, especially financially and in terms of child rearing (these difficulties are described in great detail in Ambert [1982, 1984]). It was also related to the fact that lower-SES ex-spouses were less successful at coparenting, in great part due to the desertion of fathers, as stated earlier. In comparsion, higher-SES women were more independent from their ex-husbands and could afford to be indifferent to a far greater extent than lower-SES women.

There were significant differences (beyond $p < .05$) in feelings for the ex-spouse depending on the presence of children. These differences were the same for both genders and have been amalgamated, although it should be pointed out that men showed larger differences than women. Thus, 52% of the nonparents compared to 22% of the parents felt indifference toward their ex-spouse. Moreover, 50% of the parents felt friendliness compared to 23% of the nonparents. The parents were also somewhat more likely to be angry or to dislike the ex-spouse than the nonparents. These differences between parents and nonparents stem in great part from the frustrating and often failing interdependence as parents. These differences stem in part also from the briefer marriages and the financial independence of the nonparents.

How did the respondents perceive their ex-spouse's feelings towards them? There were no important gender differences. But lower-SES men perceived their ex-wife as disliking them more than did the higher-SES men (33% vs. 12%), and this was quite an accurate perception because lower-SES women did have more negative feelings toward their ex-husband. There were very large differences in perception depending on parental status with over 72% of the nonparents but only 40% of the parents not knowing what their ex-spouse's feelings were. More parents than childless persons felt that the ex-spouse liked them or disliked them, with men reporting more perceived dislike. It is interesting to note that few respondents chose the indifference alternative in perception; instead, they chose the "I don't know how he/she feels about me" alternative.

FEELINGS TOWARD EX-SPOUSE: THE DYADIC PERSPECTIVE

I compared each ex-spouse's *stated* feelings toward the other with the other's *perception* of what those feelings might be. In view of the large number of respondents who rarely had contact with their ex-spouse, it is not surprising that 48.2% of the women and 47.1% of the men (Tables III.5 and III.6 respectively) did not know their ex-spouse's feelings towards them. Indeed, the fewer the contacts, the greater the likelihood of not knowing how one's ex-spouse felt ($p < .002$). It is also noted in Tables III.5 and III.6 that respondents were most likely to be ignorant of the ex-spouse's feelings when the ex-spouse was in reality indifferent or somewhat antagonistic toward the perceiver, in part an artifact of infrequent contacts. Conversely, comparatively few subjects responded "I don't know" when the ex-spouse had expressed a feeling of friendliness. A last comparison of the data in Tables III.5 and III.6 shows no gender difference in accuracy of perception of the ex-spouse's feeling for self: 31.8% of the men's and 29% of the women had correctly guessed their feelings for them.

In Table III.7, I went one step further and compared actual feelings for each other (along the same pattern as we had done earlier for the quality of the relationship). Fifty-four percent of the ex-couples held reciprocal feelings (Table III.7). That is, in 54% of the ex-couples, both ex-spouses held similar feelings toward each other.

In a separate analysis not presented in tabular form, I then attempted to see if congruent ex-spouses would be more accurate in perceiving each other's feelings than ex-spouses whose feelings for each other were noncongruent. The results, using alternatively men and women as the perceivers, indicated that there was no difference in the proportion of persons who did not know their ex-spouse's feelings: about 50% of men and women belonging to congruent and incongruent dyads did not know. Therefore,

Table III.5. Ex-Wives' Perceptions of Their Ex-Husbands' Feelings Toward Them Compared to the Ex-Husbands' Actual Feelings

Ex-Husbands' Actual Feelings	Misses Me	Friendly	As Happy Not To See	Dislikes Me	Indifferent	Doesn't Know His Feelings	Row Totals
			Ex-Wives' Evaluation				
Misses ex-wife		1 100.0* 5.5** 1.2***					1 1.2%
Feels friendly toward ex-wife	1 5.6 100.0 1.2	13 72.2 72.2 15.7	2 11.1 25.0 2.4			2 11.1 5.0 2.4	18 21.7%
As happy not to see ex-wife		2 6.7 11.1 2.4	4 13.3 50.0 4.8	7 23.3 50.0 8.4	1 3.3 50.0 1.2	16 53.3 40.0 19.3	30 36.1%
Dislikes ex-wife			1 9.1 12.5 1.2	6 54.5 42.9 7.2		4 36.4 10.0 4.8	11 13.3%
Feels indifferent toward ex-wife		1 4.5 5.6 1.2	1 4.5 12.5 1.2	1 4.5 7.1 1.2	1 4.5 50.0 1.2	18 81.8 45.0 21.7	22 26.5%
Doesn't know how he feels		1 100.0 5.6 1.2					1 1.2%
Column Totals	1 1.2%	18 21.7%	8 9.6%	14 16.9%	2 2.4%	40 48.2%	83 100%

Notes: * Ex-Husbands' percentage. ** Ex-Wives' percentage. *** Total percentage.

40

Table III.6. Ex-Husbands' Perceptions of their Ex-Wives' Feelings Toward Them Compared to the Ex-Wives' Actual Feelings

Ex-Wives' Actual Feelings	Ex-Husbands' Perceptions						Row Totals
	Misses Me	Friendly	As Happy Not See Me	Dislikes Me	Indifferent	Doesn't Know Her Feelings	
Misses ex-husband		2 / 66.7* / 12.5** / 2.4***				1 / 33.3 / 2.5 / 1.2	3 / 3.5%
Feels friendly toward ex-husband	1 / 6.3 / 100.0 / 1.2	10 / 62.5 / 62.5 / 11.8	1 / 6.3 / 14.3 / 1.2			4 / 25.0 / 10.0 / 4.7	16 / 18.8%
As happy not to see ex-husband		1 / 4.5 / 6.3 / 1.2	5 / 22.7 / 71.4 / 5.9	5 / 22.7 / 29.4 / 5.9	2 / 9.1 / 50.0 / 2.4	9 / 40.9 / 22.5 / 10.6	22 / 25.9%
Dislikes ex-husband		1 / 5.0 / 6.3 / 1.2		10 / 50.0 / 58.8 / 11.8		9 / 45.0 / 22.5 / 10.6	20 / 23.5%
Feels indifferent toward ex-husband		2 / 8.3 / 12.5 / 2.4	1 / 4.2 / 14.3 / 1.2	2 / 8.3 / 11.8 / 2.4	2 / 8.3 / 50.0 / 2.4	17 / 70.8 / 42.5 / 20.0	24 / 28.2%
Doesn't know how she feels							
Column Totals	1 / 1.2%	16 / 18.8%	7 / 8.2%	17 / 20.0%	4 / 4.7%	40 / 47.1%	85 / 100%

Notes: * Ex-Husbands' percentage. ** Ex-Wives' percentage. *** Total percentage.

41

Table III.7. Congruence of Feelings in Dyads: Ex-Wives' Feelings for Ex-Husbands Compared to Ex-Husbands' Feelings for Ex-Wives

Ex-Husbands' Feelings for Ex-Wives	Ex-Wives' Feelings for Ex-Husbands					Row Totals
	Misses Him	Friendly	As Happy Not See Him	Dislikes Him	Indifferent	
Misses Her					1 — 100.0	1
Friendly	1 — 5.6* — 33.3** — 1.2	11 — 61.1 — 73.3 — 13.3	3 — 16.7 — 13.6 — 3.6	1 — 5.6 — 5.3 — 1.2	2 — 11.1 — 8.3 — 2.4	18 — 21.7%
As happy not to see her	2 — 6.7 — 66.7 — 2.4	2 — 6.7 — 13.3 — 2.4	13 — 43.3 — 59.1 — 15.7	7 — 23.3 — 36.8 — 8.4	6 — 20.0 — 25.0 — 7.2	30 — 36.1%
Dislikes her			1 — 9.1 — 4.5 — 1.2	8 — 72.7 — 42.1 — 9.6	2 — 18.2 — 8.3 — 2.4	11 — 13.3%
Indifferent		1 — 4.5 — 6.7 — 1.2	5 — 22.7 — 22.7 — 6.0	3 — 13.6 — 15.8 — 3.6	13 — 59.1 — 54.2 — 15.7	22 — 26.5%
Doesn't know how he feels		1 — 100.0 — 6.7 — 1.2				1 — 1.2%
Column Totals	3 — 3.6%	15 — 18.1%	22 — 26.5%	19 — 22.9%	24 — 28.9%	83 — 100.0%

Notes: * Ex-Husbands' percentage. ** Ex-Wives' percentage. *** Total percentage.

42

congruence of actual feelings did not lessen uncertainty or increase accuracy of perception, contrary to what I had expected. Rather, it was the *type* of congruence which mattered in this respect. Thus, both for men and women, there were more accurate perceptions when both ex-spouses liked each other, and to a lesser extent, when they both disliked each other. All the women belonging to dyads congruent on friendliness ($N = 11$) correctly guessed their ex-husbands' feelings for them while 9 of the 11 ex-husbands did so. However, only half of the women belonging to dyads congruent on dislike ($N=8$) correctly guessed their ex- husbands' feelings, while 6 of the 8 husbands did so. Were these results replicated on a larger sample, they might indicate that ex-wives perceive feelings more accurately in an atmosphere of congeniality (with more contacts) while ex-husbands may be more perspicacious in an atmosphere of all-out animosity (with fewer contacts).

FEELINGS AND QUALITY OF RELATIONSHIP

If we compare Table III.3 with Table III.7, less dyadic agreement is found over feelings than over the quality of the relationship—even though feelings were more stable over time than quality of the relationship. This may stem from the more personal nature of feelings; in contrast, a relationship may be more governed by external contingencies and, as such, benefit from more obvious social markers which would make it more easily categorizable. A second reason for the greater dyadic congruence in terms of the relationship is that at least 27% of the ex-dyads had no relationship. In fact, in 31.8% of the ex-couples, at least one ex-spouse stated that no relationship existed.

It could be logically assumed that ex-dyads who hold friendly feelings will also have a friendly relationship and those who hold antagonistic feelings would have an unfriendly relationship. In order to investigate this, I identified all the ex-dyads falling within these categories in order to see what kind of overlap existed between congruence on feelings and congruence on the quality of the relationship. First, I found that 10 of the 11 ex-dyads who were congruent on feelings of friendliness were also congruent in having a friendly relationship. (The eleventh dyad believed that their relationship was "sometimes friendly.") The ex-dyads who had a friendly relationship but did not share friendly feelings were all incongruent in terms of feelings and even included one ex-spouse who disliked the other and three who felt indifferent. However, it is noteworthy that *no* ex-dyad was *congruent* in a friendly relationship *and* congruent on dislike, avoidance or even indifferent in terms of feelings. Of the eight ex-dyads congruent on feelings of dislike, six had an unfriendly relationship, one had no relationship, and the other was slightly noncongruent.

On the other hand, there were 17 ex-dyads with an unfriendly relationship: 6 were congruent on feelings of dislike, as just seen; 5 were congruent on feelings of distance-animosity; 6 were noncongruent in terms of feelings and generally included one ex-spouse who disliked the other and one who was "as happy not to see the other."

Of the 3 ex-dyads who felt indifference toward each other, 11 had no relationship. However, there were 23 ex-dyads that were congruent on no relationship. What were the remaining 12 composed of? Three ex-dyads were happy if they did not see each other, and one was congruent on dislike; the other 7 were noncongruent on feelings but only slightly so and these feelings were of indifference, avoidance, anger, or dislike.

Generally, congruence on the quality of a relationship between ex-spouses follows the feelings each ex-spouse have for the other. Ex-dyads who dislike each other do not have a friendly relationship. Similarly, those who like each other do not have a conflictual relationship. *Congruence on feelings had a greater impact on congruence of relationship than vice versa.*

In terms of the *evolution of feelings* over time, only three persons indicated a change in their feelings for their ex-spouse since separation from dislike to like and none from like to dislike. When a shift occurred, it was from one of these two (like or dislike) in the direction of any of the other milder options which, in themselves, were not related to frequency of contacts.[2] However, in terms of the quality of the *relationship*, ten persons indicated having a more cordial relationship now than was the case at the beginning of the separation. As well, more persons had "no relationship" than used to be the case early on in the separation. But these shifts in the quality and even the existence of the relationship were no necessarily accompanied by a shift in feelings: as previously shown feelings were stable over time. What changes over time is the frequency of contacts and the structure of the relationship—or even the existence of the relationship.

TYPES OF EX-COUPLES

Because there were so few ex-couples who were mutually friendly (11 or only 13% of all ex-couples; see Table III.7), I wanted to know if anything differentiated them from "angry" ex-couples or even "indifferent" ex-couples. The rationale behind this inquiry was that congruent, friendly ex-couples will function much more adequately as coparents than embattled ex-couples or even those who express indifference for each other. I found that, in a majority of the cases (90%), both friendly and disliking ex-couples had children, while only 46% of the indifferent ex-couples were parents. Ex-couples who disliked each other scored two points lower than friendly ex-couples in their evaluation of their past marriage (on a 5-point scale, $p < .000$).[3] A more difficult and stormier marriage was also described by the disliking couples in the conversational material. The data for the 98 longitudinal respondents indicated that a stormy and unhappy marriage led to feelings of anger and dislike (and even indifference) after separation. Women in particular were very vocal in pointing out that a miserable marriage could only lead to ill feelings after divorce or, at the very least, indifference. It is also noteworthy that *respondents were very consistent over several years in repeated evaluations of their past marriage.*

Friendly ex-dyads (both in terms of feelings as well as of relationship) saw each other regularly or never saw each other in one case of a brief marriage devoid of animosity. Ex-couples congruent on dislike saw each other rarely or occasionally. Only one embattled ex-couple saw each other frequently. Therefore, feelings of friendliness were related to frequent contacts but feelings of animosity were related to somewhat more distant contacts *when ex-spouses were congruent.* The statistical data and the conversational material both indicated that feelings influenced contacts. In turn, post-marital contacts or lack of contacts reinforced or sustained these feelings.

Both men and women in friendly ex-couples showed a very high level of satisfaction with their children: on a 5-point scale, they scored 4.6 while, in the dislike ex-couples, men's satisfaction was 3.7 and women's 3.3.[4] The friendly ex-spouses tended to express a more positive attitude toward their ex-affines, while the unfriendly ex-couples expressed negative feelings or said that no relationship existed between them and their ex-parents-in-law. Consequently, children of friendly ex-couples did benefit, not only from a more harmonious coparental arrangement, but from a more harmonious and continuous relationship with their grandparents as well (Ambert 1988).

A last result to be reported here is that the ex-couples who were congruent on friendliness were more frequently homogeneous in terms of SES, whether at a higher SES or a lower SES.[5] In contrast, ex-couples congruent on dislike as well as on an unfriendly relationship, not only were less homogeneous, but were more often of lower SES as well. The cases of heterogeneity usually stemmed from a woman's downward mobility following the separation, and such a situation exacerbated tension: these men's standard of living did not go down after separation, while women's did.

TYPES OF EX-COUPLES: CASE STUDIES

In this section, case studies will be presented of ex-couples congruent on friendliness and ex-couples holding negative feelings for each other. The ex-couples herein introduced were chosen on the basis of how typical they were of the others in their particular category. Ex-couples who held positive feelings toward each other will be discussed first.

Ray Dodge, age 45, is a Bell supervisor and his ex-wife, Diana Martin, age 44 works with her second husband of five years in his small business.[6] Ray and Diana had two girls during their 16-year marriage and both young women are now married. One daughter had a child and was expecting another at the time of the last interview. Before her remarriage, Diana had been a secretary. Both ex-spouses come from upper-lower-class Catholic backgrounds.

Ray was interviewed three times (1979, 1981, 1984), and his reports on his relationship with his ex-wife have been consistently good. Her reports in 1981 and 1984 were similar. Neither blamed the other for the end of their marriage. "I think we got married too soon and I'm glad the children waited longer" (Ray). Both held a positive opinion of each other. She described him as "honest, hard working, kind, a good father. I still like him. We talk over the phone once in a while and he drops in occasionally. My husband thinks I'm lucky because he is always fighting with his ex-wife." When asked how Ray would describe her, she said: "That I am good mother and a good woman. I don't hold grudges. I'm a hard worker." Ray concurred during his interview: "She's a nice woman. Warm hearted type. She's nice, good temper, good disposition."

After 10 years of separation, they see each other every other month and converse on the phone four or five times a year. As he points out, "With both children married, one grandchild and another on the way, we've got more opportunities of running into each other." Their marriage had been largely devoid of conflict and the decision to separate was arrived at mutually. After that, Ray had contributed fairly to the support of their children.

Ray spends most of his spare time reconditioning cars with a group of friends—a hobby which already used to keep him away from home a great deal while married. He dates occasionally and his "buddies" often "fix" him up "with girls for one-night stands." He is not interested in remarrying. Throughout the interviews, Ray was matter of fact, straightforward, uncomplicated. In 1981, I noted down: "Intelligent, friendly and open. As normal as can be." Diana was quite similar. In 1979, their children appeared pleasant, warm, and uncomplicated. Both parents were pleased with their daughters, pleased with each other as parents, and close to their children. Diana was very happy in her remarriage and so was her second husband. Both Ray and her second husband appreciated each other and felt quite comfortable. Diana's two stepchildren, also married, with small children were getting along very well with her and these stepchildren socialized a great deal with her own children. Theirs was an extended family system. (Ray and Diana are described further in Chapter IV.)

The second ex-couple on friendly terms share many similarities with Diana and Ray, in spite of differences in lifestyle. Sean and Deirde Flannigan, age 43 and 42 respectively, have three teenagers from their 16-year marriage. Separated for five years, Sean remarried three years ago to a 33-year-old nurse who has custody of her 8-year-old daughter. Sean, Deirde, and the new wife are all

Catholic. Sean is a reasonably well-to-do tax consultant and Deirde is a high-ranking personal secretary.

Sean initiated the separation: "My first marriage never took. It never felt right. My wife was a very nice person and it wasn't a mistake in choosing the wrong person, it was just not the right chemistry. We had a nice family, a nice house, but we weren't too affectionate, we didn't do too many things together." He felt very unhappy while she was fairly happy. When he decided to separate, Deirde says that "he insisted that we sit down and draw up a separation plan. We were both very upset but that's the way it had to go. Of course, I would have preferred it if we could have survived."

Deirde took custody of the three children; "the house, the car, and [Sean] promised always to support the children [...] by that time we had calmed down and I said, 'Look, I'll be here next weekend to fix the leak if there is one!'" Both said that they quarreled a great deal at first but "we put up a front for the children and our families and we got carried away and ended up pretty good friends." After he remarried, their daughter, now age 19, moved in with him because she could not study at her mother's home because "one of my [brothers] is in the school band and the other is always playing video games." Both parents were positive about this move. Both have always been supportive of each other as parents. They see each other once a month and talk over the phone once a month. Their conversations are broad-ranging and not restricted.

Sean is now very happily remarried. His new wife and his ex-wife get along very well. Deirde: "His wife has made a new man out of him [...] In a way yes, I am jealous of him, not of her, because I'd like to be remarried to someone as supportive as she is but men like that don't exist." Sean: "This may be unusual but we get along much better since I've remarried because my wife has been very good to her [ex-wife] and to the children, and my ex-wife doesn't feel threatened. It is as if she had gained a new friend ... There has been no jealousy." Sean's little stepdaughter, according to his new wife, "adores her big sister [step-sister] and she loves it when the boys come over. Sometimes she goes along with her sister when she visits her mother." Sean and his new wife live only four blocks away from Deirde. The new wife: "It's so convenient for the older children. They can visit and still see their friends." She and Deirde see each other every other week, at times at the bus stop or at the supermarket. The new wife: "No, we don't socialize as such, but we are friendly and we get along ... She's a nice person." (The new wife herself has a very negative relationship with her own ex-husband and her case is presented later in this chapter.) Both Sean and Deirde were easy to interview; they were pleasant.

There were common threads running through these two vignettes, and these themes were generally characteristic of the other friendly ex-couples: homogeneous backgrounds, no or little feminine downward mobility, little marital conflict, fair separation agreement and continued paternal financial support, close parent-child relationships on both sides, coparenting, good mutual assessment as persons and as parents by the ex-spouses, excellent remarriages, functional relationships between new spouse and ex-spouse of the remarried person, maintenance of relationship with ex-affines, mature personalities, and establishment of an extended kin system after remarriage. These common threads were also found among a limited number of ex-couples whose feelings for each other were noncongruent: one ex-spouse was indifferent while the other was friendly. However, these characteristics were not met as a group in other types of ex-couples. Psychologists could say that these characteristics constitute a cluster that would be factorially related to such a type of ex-couples and, as it is called here, to a successful divorce.

However, the two ex-couples described had children (90% of the friendly ex-couples had children). For the *childless* ex-couples, successful divorces were also encountered when there was congruence on indifference or noncongruence on indifference/friendly, indifference/as happy not see the other: the absence of children did not lead to the necessity for a relationship after the separation. Thus, the post-marital situation was quite different structurally. The two ex-couples described above represented successful divorces *for persons with children. Successful divorces for the childless have fewer requirements.* Nevertheless, the fact remains that 50% of divorces include children and over one-third of noncustodial parents rarely if ever see their children two years after divorce. Therefore, in terms of social consequences, discussion of ex-couples with children is more important, and the two vignettes represent what ought to be a norm while, in reality, they are exceptions. As Ahrons points out, couples rarely divorce well.

The second part of this section deals with ex-couples who have negative feelings for each other. The first case involves Sean's new wife, Kathy, a 33-year-old nurse who has custody of her 8-year-old daughter. Remarried three years ago, she had been separated from her former husband, Harry Bishop, for five years. Harry is a 36-year-old executive with a M.B.A. degree. He is Protestant; Kathy converted to Catholicism before remarrying Sean. Two years ago, Harry remarried the 28-year-old ex-wife of a well-to-do financier. His new wife comes from an affluent background and has custody of her 5-year-old son. Therefore, Harry has a live-in stepson while his own young daughter lives with his ex-wife Kathy.

Harry was interviewed three times (1979, 1981, 1984). He had suffered from a demotion at work in 1981. He rated his relationship with Kathy as average in 1979 and 1981 but as below average in 1984. Kathy herself rates it as average, and both agree that they would rather not see each other. In 1981, he was depressed and cried about his little daughter during the interview: "They do not trust me with her, but I am not dangerous. I am just a very depressed man when I have problems. My little girl is really a stranger, I can't be a father. I have lost even that. I have nothing worthwhile." (He had spent some time in a psychiatric ward that year.) In my notes in 1981, I described him as "sweet, overly sensitive, not terribly assertive, attractive."

He had a great deal of recriminations over the demise of his marriage, as Kathy had decided to separate, not he: "We had many problems but we have more now. So what was the point? ... She wanted a different me and that can't easily occur. She was too demanding ... She's told me that I was unstable, that I could never understand a woman." Kathy also believes that she does not treat Harry as well as she should; she agreed that, in their marriage, she was the decision maker. Yet, she is not a particularly aggressive or assertive person: "My former husband was a big child and I just wasn't coping too well with that type of person. It was too stressful."

She is very happy in her remarriage and so is her new husband, as we saw previously. Harry, however, described his remarriage as somewhat unhappy: "My wife is spoiled and I wish she'd go out and work ... Her parents give her money, her ex-husband gives her money and I give her money. She just does her own little thing." His new wife was rather unpleasant during *her* interview. Her little boy was hyperactive. Harry believes he made a mistake in marrying her and feels she could leave him "any minute." However, from the contents of her interview, his fears are unfounded as his new wife has a good life, if not a good marriage.

The problem between Kathy and Harry is their daughter whom Harry sees only three or four times a year. Kathy: "He doesn't know how to handle it [fatherhood] but the main problem is that she was so small when we separated that she doesn't feel any attachment while he does. And I started dating my [new] husband quite a while ago and he is all she can remember. She is growing up normally under unusual circumstances." The little girl is a pleasant well-behaved child. She calls her stepfather Daddy. We also saw in a previous vignette that she was very fond of her step-siblings. Once in a while Harry asks to talk to the child over the phone. The little girl, however, does not know what to say. Kathy coparents efficiently and her family is a very affectionate one. The problem for the ex-spouses is that she does not coparent with her ex-husband, the child's father, but with the child's stepfather. Harry: "I am always the one who calls. Her mother does not encourage her to do so, so you can't expect a child this young to maintain a relationship with someone she hasn't lived with since she was a baby." In turn, Harry does not have a good rapport with his step-son, although he is very fond of him: "His father takes him each weekend and calls him practically everyday so I don't have much of a chance there and the father is even threatening to get custody of his son if we do this or if we don't do that. It's quite upsetting."

By 1984, Harry was less depressed and more assertive. Nevertheless, relationships with key females in his life were still very unrewarding. It is noteworthy that his new wife and her ex-husband's relationship was also extremely poor.

The following ex-couple also responded that they disliked each other. Esther Epstein, age 40, a part-time supervisor at a clothing store, has custody of a 15-year-old son and a 13-year-old daughter She is remarried to a pharmacist. Esther's ex-husband, Steve Goldberg, is a 42-year-old engineer, also remarried. His new wife is a 34-year-old sales executive. Esther and Steve have separated five years ago because he was having affairs. All was going well until a friend informed Esther. Esther: "I packed his suitcases and threw them to his face and told him never to come back and I filed for divorce. ... He admitted it but he said it had nothing to do with our marriage and I said it had everything to do with it." After this, she refused him access to the children for the next six months. Steve "nearly had a nervous breakdown" while Esther actually had one. Says she, "He is weak man, a sheep, he has no character." Esther and Steve see each other and talk over the phone every other week, and these communications merely exacerbate their mutual dislike. Actually, this ex-couple has the highest rate of contact among embattled ex-dyads.

Both ex-spouses agree that their children have serious problems. Esther: "I have had problems with the children ever since ... So you can understand that I have little love for my former husband. He ruined too many lives." She allows Steve access to the children simply "because of the support payments and I don't think they'll care to see him later on in life." The son has a drug-related juvenile record and the daughter is constantly truant. The daughter, in a punk-style hairdo, came home during the interview, acknowledged no one, grabbed something out of the frig, and went upstairs, after which we heard the stereo blare.

Steve: "I can't have a meaningful conversation with them or try to straighten them out because they wouldn't listen or they would complain to their mother and she would prevent them from seeing me. I can always take her to court but you must appreciate what a headache this is." Later one, he added: "I think my children were caught in the middle of our problems with her being so violently against me, it is bound to affect children negatively ... and then her family jumped in and they fried me alive, all the while in front of the children. In addition, my former wife never had much discipline, she does not know how to raise children ... So long as the children know that *I* am to blame, they're not going to put their act together."

What are the two ex-spouses' remarriages like? Esther's remarriage is, in her own words, very average (although her new husband feels fairly happy): "He is a bit unreliable, he often gets upset at my children ... well, that's what happens after a divorce; it's difficult to find the perfect man and I had to settle for less but it is better than nothing." Steve is extremely happy in his remarriage. He obviously adores his new wife; he is affectionate and she returns his affection openly. She was very nice to him and praised him openly about his patience with his ex-wife. His new wife's remarriage is, however, quite another story: she is "neither happy nor unhappy" in it. She wanted to remarry and then be free to live her own life, which she does, including having affairs while on business trips, all the while making Steve happy; "I make certain to give him moral support, I have his family over, I bring him small gifts from my trips but the rest [of my life] is all mine."

In Chapter IV, two additional ex-couples will be encountered who were antagonistic: Bruno Matieri and Mary; Janice and Joe Smith. (Janice is also further described in Chapter II as one of the welfare mothers.) By the third interview, Janice had not seen her ex-husband for three years. Neither had he seen any of his five children from her nor, for that matter, the two children from his second marriage.

Antagonistic ex-couples often had a history of adultery, desertion, and nonsupport of children on the part of fathers. Nonsupport creates more antagonism, although the reverse causality path was also encountered. Ex-couples who held negative feelings for each other did not coparent or did not do so effectively. The noncustodial parent's relationships with the children were distant, superficial, or even nonexistant. When remarried, the ex-spouses were more likely to have a less happy marriage, and the new spouse had nothing to do with the ex-spouses or was even antagonistic toward him or her as well. Generally, there was no extended family, and even relationships with ex-affines were nonexistent or strained. Emotional problems that had required treatment were very common, and in many cases one (or both) of the ex-spouses had a personality that lacked warmth, was domineering, chauvinistic, or self-centered. Moreover, these divorces frequently, although not always, were unsuccessful: not only was the family unit effectively broken by the lack of coparenting and contact with the children, but one or both ex-spouses, in addition to harboring negative feelings for each other, were not happy in their remarriage or had been unable to find a new mate (when one was wanted).

CONCLUSIONS AND DISCUSSION

In spite of discussions in the literature on the lack of institutionalization of norms regarding ex-spouses' relationships to each other, a high level of agreement was found among divorced and formerly-divorced persons concerning the normative aspect of their relationship.[7] Respondents opted for a polite form of relationship as opposed to a conflictual one or a publicly embarrassing one. However, respondents were very divided concerning *what* the actual relationship should be. The data on the actual relationship clearly indicated that this latter lack of consensus at the normative level reflected the reality. In practice, the relationship between ex-spouses was a spotty one at best, both in terms of frequency of contact and in terms of quality (Ahrons and Rodgers 1987; Duberman 1975).

Children were certainly the most significant factor in promoting the ex-spousal relationship. Unless ex-spouses were parents, they rarely saw or talked to each other. However, as in Luepnitz's study (1982), many were the respondents who felt inexorably tied down to their ex-spouse because of the children who represented a past the adults needed to leave behind after six years of separation. In contrast, a new spouse or "new" children represented the present and the future. This can be seen in the fact that many parents never saw each other, and Furstenberg and Nord (1985) similarly found that nearly half of the *children* in their study had not seen their noncustodial parent in the past year. In our study, fully one-third of the parents rarely saw each other, although this percentage was more representative of lower-SES than higher-SES persons.

One important conclusion from my data is that persons of lower SES did not pursue their coparental role as frequently or as effectively as persons with a more solid socioeconomic situation. Lower-SES fathers were much less likely to seek custody of their children, and less likely to contribute to their support. (However, an American study has found that middle-income men were as likely as low-income men not to pay child support [Weitzman 1981].) They were judged by their ex-wives as less competent parents. In this sample, children of divorce at the low end of the SES scale had experienced more behavioral problems while their parents were still married and even more after the separation than other more privileged children. Moreover, their problems had had more serious social consequences (early pregnancies, jail, foster homes, mother battering) than the problems of more privileged children.

No matter how we analyzed the data, it was obvious that post-marital harmony was a minority phenomenon. *Not only were marital problems extended into the post-marital period, but new problems arose specific to the divorce itself.* Most ex-spouses tried to distance themselves from the other (Furstenberg 1982), even though they expressed the opinion that they should stand by each other as coparents. While it is true that parents were more likely to be positive than the childless, such a harmonious feeling was nevertheless rare,especially considering the norm expressed. This hiatus between norm and reality was acknowledged by many respondents as fully 41% believed that they did not treat their ex-spouse as should be. Therefore, it would be very important to research those variables which stand between norms and their actualization. The norms may be unrealistic and mere wishful thinking. The very nature of marriage (i.e., romantic syndrome) and of the post-marital relationship in this society may well preclude the actualization of an ideal of post-marital harmony as a general rule.

In terms of feelings, the results certainly did not indicate any long-standing attachment to the ex-spouse six years post-separation (see also, Bernard 1956). Here as well, children were the pivotal variable with parents being less indifferent than nonparents, more likely to be positive *or* negative. Also, 54% of the dyads were congruent on feelings for each other. Thus, in one case out of two, ex-spouses' feelings for each other were reciprocal, although only 13% were reciprocally friendly. Moreover, there was greater congruence among the ex-pairs in terms of the quality of the relationship than in terms of feelings, although only 20% categorized their relationship as a friendly one and another 8% as occasionally friendly.

Congruent dyads at the friendly level, however few, generally had children, had more regular contacts, and were of higher SES, especially with a higher education. Let us return for an instant to the fact that higher SES persons seemed to be better able to function adequately as coparents, especially in cases of dual-career ex-spouses. As Jackson (1982) points out, there is little research available on parenting after divorce for persons of higher SES. A woman's financial self-sufficiency, I hypothesize, may be a pivotal variable in allowing for a more satisfactory coparental role. (There is a suggestion to this effect in Furstenberg and Spanier [1984, p. 115]). Financial independence promotes a sense of self-esteem and of control over life, elements which allow a woman to run her life without constantly turning to her ex-spouse for help. The latter, in turn, is able to relinquish the spousal role and to concentrate on the coparental one: he is free from his ex-wife as a wife, and vice versa. Both partners have fewer sources of conflict and can cooperate more effectively as parents.

I was particulary struck by the fact that in ex-couples who were coparenting amicably, *both* ex-spouses seemed mature, reasonably adaptable, and may have been better adjusted overall than those ex-spouses who were congruent on the negative side and were unable to coparent. Even when only one ex-spouse harbored negative feelings for the other, coparenting was not likely to succeed and the ex-spousal relationship was not a productive one. The more troubled marriages of ex-spouses who were out of "sync" had produced more difficult children as observed prospectively several years earlier; this sequence was then followed by a more embattled divorce, even after an average of six years post separation (see also, Burgoyne and Clark 1984, p. 351; Nolan 1977). Coparentally, these divorces were failures, as had been the marriages. In contrast, the mutually friendly ex-couples as well as many who were mutually indifferent, had experienced less difficult marriages which were followed by what we will call *successful divorces,* especially at the coparental level. These results indicate that successful coparenting after divorce, as well as harmonious post-divorce relationships would be important topics of research. Aside from the obvious scientific interest and the shift away from the negative aspects of divorce they represent,[8] studies of successful divorces might offer guidance to counsellors and other personnel who treat, help, or advise divorcing couples—the more so since these professionals see only those dyads (or their children) which are malfunctioning at one or several levels.

However, when there were no children or the children had been on their own for a while, at separation, the function of coparenting was not necessary. Thus, such ex-spouses did not need to cooperate with each other, *did not have forced ties to each other.* Consequently, *it is far easier for such divorces to be successful—*

provided, of course, that financial or social matters do not intervene (such as maintenance, alimony, friends in common, and so forth)—than divorces including children. *The personality requirements did not seem so demanding.* At the very least, I have observed that, for such a divorce to be successful, it needed be successful for only one person and not necessarily for both. Or, from another perspective, I have encountered ex-spouses where one held negative feelings but the other was indifferent; there was no ex-spousal relationship to speak of, but one of the two partners was very happily divorced or very happily remarried, or even both of them were. In some cases, one ex-spouse had a very problematic personality, even a long treatment career for emotional problems. But, so long as the other spouse was stable, reasonably mature and adaptable, that person generally had a successful divorce. However, had this same ex-couple shared children, the divorce would have been far less successful for *both parties* because of the difficulties created by the less stable person and the requisites to coparent which would have placed a burden on an already over-taxed ex-dyad.

To maintain or not to maintain a (good) relationship with one's ex-spouse is perhaps immaterial so long as there are no children and so long as one ex-spouse is not dependent upon the other for material or social survival. Material survival involves money mainly; social survival involves social mobility (downward) because of the divorce, dependency on the other because of a shared network of acquaintances, friends, neighbors. A further corollary is that the maintenance of a *reasonable* relationship with the ex-spouse will be more necessary in a smaller community than in a metropolis and more necessary in a self-contained, relatively close social world, as in the case of a small minority group or a very interconnected professional environment. Ex-spouses from a cohesive minority group may have additional difficulties in being allowed to get a fresh start on their own terms. A secondary corollary is that geographical distance may contribute to the success of a divorce when there are no children.

From another angle, I have observed that there were more persons who had a *successful divorce* among the *childless* and the *financially independent* than among those who had had children and/or were impoverished. It may be said here that one of the reasons may be the relatively short-lived marriage rather than the absence of children or of financial solvency. This may well be true in most cases but there still were short-lived marriages which had produced children (and they were unsuccessful divorces) as well as a few long-lived childless marriages with no financial dependence which were successful. *Dependency on the other ex-spouse, whether for child-rearing, money, or social considerations is not conducive to peace after a divorce.*

There are, therefore, practical implications, especially for women, in such a conclusion. Indeed, women are generally more dependent economically and socially than men, and this is especially so when they have children. Studies have shown that divorce can depress a mother's income by some 70% while her husband's standard of living may go up by 40% (Hewlett 1986). Therefore, for women, there is a financial inequity in divorce which can only exacerbate tensions between ex-spouses. However, the financially independent mother, as we have seen in earlier data, is more likely to have a successful divorce than the one who depends on her husband for child support and maintenance. I will add here that this is made possible because such a woman is able to bear the entire burden of childcare and, often, child support. Her successful divorce and especially that of her ex-spouse is based on a principle of inequity in many instances. Thus, although the ex-spousal relationship allows for a great deal of variety, there are certain social and even demographic constraints that may prolong it, exacerbate it, or facilitate it.

NOTES

1.   This chapter, focuses on the 212 subjects with ex-spouses still living: 163 were remarried and 49 were still divorced. This total includes 85 ex-dyads. (In the entire study, one couple remarried each other after a 4-year separation, including a 1-year divorce. They are excluded from this chapter.) The 85 ex-couples included in this analysis were composed of persons who had been married to each other in a *first* marriage. Second ($N = 19$) and third ($N = 3$) dissolved marriages (for the multiply-divorced persons) were excluded because of the programming complexity (and cost) involved in the matching of ex- spouses other than the first for *both* ex-partners. However, 17 of the 19 multiply-divorced persons are included herein for their first marriage. Multiply-divorced persons and their ex-spouses are discussed in Chapter V.

2.   On shifts of feelings overtime, see Hetherington et al. (1978) and Kitson (1982).

3. "All in all, how happy was your previous marriage for you?" (5 = very happy; 1 = very unhappy). This question forms one of the focuses of the next chapter.

4. "All in all, how satisfied are you with your children's behavior?" (very satisfied = 5; very dissatisfied = 1). Systematic observations carried out in 1978-1980 on the children of 6 of these congruent ex-couples (4 friendly and 2 unfriendly ex-couples) had indicated from a prospective viewpoint that the children whose parents had had a less stormy marriage and who were friendly in 1984 had been less difficult than children of the "dislike" ex-couples. Already in 1978-1980, parents were more satisfied with their children when, in 1984, they were to express friendliness toward each other than those expressing dislike.

5. The results for the ex-couples congruent on indifference tended to fall between those of the friendly and disliking ex-couples.

6. In the case studies, all names are fictive. In certain cases, in order to further ensure anonymity, a respondent's occupation has been changed for another occupation at a same level. In a few instances the gender and even age of the children has been changed.

7. One key result of this study (which cannot be discussed at length for the sake of parsimony) resides in that ex-husbands and ex- wives *within* dyads gave nearly identical responses to these normative questions, as well as to the questions pertaining to frequency of contacts. This result indicates that certain types of information can be as accurately obtained from one spouse or, in this case, one ex-spouse as from the other (Thomson and Williams 1983; however, see Reitig and Bubolz 1983). This note can be entered in the discussion on the reliance of one respondent in family research (reviewed in Bokemeier and Monroe 1983); however, the remainder of my data clearly indicates the need for more research involving both partners (see Thompson and Walker 1982), especially in studies of divorce.

8. On this, see Kitson and Raschke (1981) as well as Kraus (1981).

Chapter IV

Past and Current
Marital Happiness

Oh, I was so, so unhappy with him, you have no idea. He has no idea either.
—Woman, unskilled worker

Marital happiness is not something which is as concrete for a man as it is for a woman. [... ?] It's something we feel, we live whereas men's lives are focused elsewhere.
—Woman, teacher

My marriage is happy. It's got to be happy otherwise why would I have remarried?
—Man, mid-level executive

The focus of this chapter is on couples' perception of their past marriage and current marriage. The questions to be addressed first are: How do ex-spouses evaluate their past marital happiness? How do these same persons perceive their current marital happiness, when remarried? These are followed by: How happy do they perceive their marriage to have been for their ex-spouse? How happy do the new spouses perceive their marriage to be for their new husband/wife? Case vignettes of ex-spouses who had been happy in their previous marriage are presented and compared with others who had been unhappy. The same approach is then followed for remarried couples.

MARITAL HAPPINESS: OVERVIEW

The literature generally indicates that respondents tend to rate their marital happiness rather highly, but that women, including divorced women rating their previous marriage, are always more negative than men (Hetherington 1987; Singh et al. 1978; Veroff et al. 1981). This has led Jessie Bernard (1973) to posit a "his" and a "hers" perceptive of marriage as well as to advance the theory that marriage is a more advantageous state for men than for women.

Moreover, studies have shown that respondents at a higher level of the socioeconomic scale (SES) report greater marital happiness than respondents at the lower end. As Veroff et al. (1981, p. 391) point out: "We might suggest that a happy marriage leads to higher income, but it is more compelling to see higher income leading to marital happiness." Marital happiness has also been studied in conjunction with the stages of the life cycle (Lupri and Frideres 1981; Rollins and Cannon 1974; Spanier et al. 1975; Weishaus and Field 1988). The results show a curvilinear relationship with the highest level of marital happiness found among recently married persons and those at the "empty-nest" stage; the lowest levels of marital happiness occur among childrearing individuals (Steinberg and Silverberg 1987).

This chapter will begin with the individuals; the couple perspective is examined later. The Time 3 or 1984 results of two questions—"How happy was your first marriage for you?" and "How happy was your first marriage for your ex-husband [or ex-wife]?"—will be utilized. The alternatives ranged from very happy = 1 to very unhappy = 5. The questionnaire contained many other questions on marital happiness and adjustment. Only one is retained here, not only to simplify the presentation but also because this question was the one highly correlated with the others most consistently. It was the best indicator of a person's overall evaluation of his/her marital happiness.[1] The second question on the perception of the ex-spouse's past marital happiness is not generally included in studies of divorce. In addition, the couple or dyadic approach of this study allows the comparison of one spouse's perception of the other's happiness with this person's actual feelings. Many additional analyses can be carried out with these two questions in conjunction with many others. But these are more suitable for journal articles. The purpose of this chapter is to present an overview as well as case studies.

Table IV. 1. Marital Happiness and Perception of Spouse's Marital Happiness in Current and Previous Marriages

	Current Marriages (remarriages)				Previous Marriages			
	Husbands		Wives		Ex-Husbands		Ex-Wives	
	$\bar{X}$	(N)	$\bar{X}$	(N)	$\bar{X}$	(N)	$\bar{X}$	(%)
Marital happiness	1.56*	(101)	1.75	(103)	3.00	(102)	3.52	(110)
Perception of spouse's marital happiness	1.38	(101)	1.36	(103)	2.86	(97)	2.61	(110)
	%	(N)	%	(N)	%	(N)	%	(N)
Marital happiness								
Very	65.3	(66)	57.3	(59)	8.8	(9)	5.5	(6)
Fairly	16.8	(17)	20.4	(21)	23.5	(24)	20.9	(23)
Neither	13.9	(14)	13.6	(14)	36.3	(37)	20.9	(23)
Fairly unhappy	4.0	(4)	7.8	(8)	21.6	(22)	21.8	(24)
Very unhappy	0.0	(0)	1.0	(1)	9.8	(10)	30.9	(34)
Perception								
Very	73.3	(74)	72.8	(75)	7.2	(7)	4.5	(5)
Fairly	17.8	(18)	18.4	(19)	27.8	(27)	40.0	(44)
Neither	6.9	(7)	8.7	(9)	39.2	(38)	45.5	(50)
Fairly unhappy	2.0	(2)	0.0	(0)	23.7	(23)	10.0	(11)
Very unhappy	0.0	(0)	0.0	(0)	2.1	(2)	0.0	(0)

Note: Very happy = 1; very unhappy = 5.

In Table IV.1, we present the results in the form of averages (top panel) and in percentages for each alternative chosen (bottom panel). Current marriages (left-hand segment), not unexpectedly, are perceived as being very to fairly happy, while past marriages (right-hand segment) are reported to have been relatively unhappy. Nevertheless, we see that nearly 30% of the ex-spouses recall their previous marriage as having been very to fairly happy (26% of the ex-wives versus 32% of the ex-husbands). Yet, this happy marriage has been terminated. This will lead to study differences that may exist between happily-married couples who divorce and those who divorce after a rather unhappy marriage in a later section. "Common sense" dictates that divorce occurs only when marriages are unhappy, not happy. Where is the anomaly? Why do happily married persons divorce?

Another way of looking at the information provided in Table IV.1 is to examine gender differences. More men than women saw their previous marriage as having been neither happy nor unhappy: 36% versus 23% of the women. However, 53% of all ex-wives reported a fairly to very unhappy marriage in comparison to only 30% of the ex-husbands. It is significant that, in the interviews, women gave more causes for their divorce than men; they also expressed more dissatisfaction with most aspects of their previous marriage than men. They had more complaints and reported more disagreements than men did. This could be interpreted to mean that their past marriage had indeed been far unhappier and/or that they were more perspicacious or more willing to complain. The data support all three possibilities.

The gender difference was much smaller, and nonsignificant statistically, for current marriages. Even here, twice as many women than men (8.8% versus 4%) described themselves as fairly to very unhappy in their remarriage. Overall, as in other studies, men were happier than women and reported fewer areas of disagreement and tension than women (White 1979). Fewer men than women estimated that they would not be married to their current spouse in ten years hence. In the conversational data, more women made comments about having had to "settle for less," either because of their age and/or the urgency of their financial difficulties. The men in this study had not "settled for less," or, at least, did not admit having done so.

When asked to evaluate their ex-spouse's past marital happiness, both men and women gave it a higher evaluation than to their own. In other words, *divorced persons saw their ex-spouse as having been far happier than they had themselves been.* As indicated by the figures presented earlier, it is obvious that only the women were correct in this evaluation—up to a point. It is clear that a large gap exists between ex-husbands' perceptions and ex-wives' reality. This point will be further discussed.

In terms of current marriages, the gap between perception and reported reality was far smaller than for past marriages. Nevertheless, there was a tendency to overestimate one's spouse's happiness in comparison to one's own and in comparison to the spouse's own evaluation. Once again, men overestimated their wife's happiness more than did their wife. Moreover, wives still perceived a larger gap between their own happiness and that of their husband than husbands did between their *own* happiness and that of their wife.

THE QUESTION OF SOCIAL CLASS

As indicated in Chapter II, social class has proven to be a key determining variable in my research on divorce. This section will look at class and gender. In Table IV.2, the respondents' past and current marital happiness by class is shown in the left hand columns. Lower-SES women had the worse score of all six categories of persons in terms of past marital happiness while all three categories of men had better scores than all three categories of women. Thus, *being a woman and being a lower-SES woman insured a low level of past marital happiness.* In the right-hand columns, respondents' perception of their ex-spouse's past marital happiness is presented. Lower-SES ex-husbands, although far apart in their scores of *perception* from their ex-wives' reality, nevertheless perceived their ex-wives to have been unhappier (3.29) than they themselves had been (2.40). Of all the ex-husbands, they gave (quite rightly so) their wives the worse scores. Lower-SES ex-wives, on the other hand, perceived their ex-husbands to have been unhappier than their ex-husbands perceived themselves, perhaps a reaction to the depth of these women's own past unhappiness.

Lower-SES women had also the lowest level of happiness in their current marriage and so did lower-SES men. However, the spread in happiness was larger among women, from 1.40 for higher-SES women to 2.22 for lower-SES women, than for men: 1.49 for higher-SES men compared to 2.00 for lower-SES men. There was practically no difference between men and women at the higher-SES level, indicating the determining importance of SES in terms of marital happiness.

Similarly, lower-SES persons also perceived their spouses as being unhappier than did higher-SES persons. Here as well, lower-SES wives perceived their husbands as less happy (1.67) than the husbands perceived themselves (2.00). The reverse occurred among lower-SES husbands' perceptions: they perceived their wives as happier than the wives perceived themselves.

Table IV.2.. Current and Past Marital Happiness and Perception
of Spouse's and Ex-spouses Marital Happiness by SES

	Respondent's Happiness in Previous Marriage		Perception of Ex-spouse's Happiness in Previous Marriage	
	(N)	$\bar{X}$	*(N)*	$\bar{X}$
Ex-husbands	(102)	3.00*	(97)	2.86
Upper SES	(50)	2.82	(47)	2.60
Middle SES	(37)	3.08	(36)	3.03
Lower	(15)	2.40	(14)	3.29
Ex-wives	(110)	3.52	(110)	2.61
Upper SES	(41)	3.39	(41)	2.58
Middle SES	(50)	3.42	(50)	2.54
Lower SES	(19)	4.05	(19)	2.84
	Repondent's Happiness in Current Marriage		Perception of Ex-spouse's Happiness in Current Marriage	
	(N)	$\bar{X}$	*(N)*	$\bar{X}$
Husbands	(101)	1.56	(101)	1.38
Upper SES	(53)	1.49	(53)	1.28
Middle SES	(40)	1.58	(40)	1.43
Lower	(8)	2.00	(8)	1.75
Wives	(103)	1.75	(103)	1.36
Upper SES	(42)	1.40	(42)	1.19
Middle SES	(52)	1.94	(52)	1.44
Lower SES	(9)	2.22	(9)	1.67

Note: * Very happy = 1; very unhappy = 5.

All data, whether qualitative or quantitative, indicated that membership in the lower class brought about marriages which were unhappier than marriages in the other classes. This was so especially in terms of marriages that had ended in divorce, and especially so for women of the lower class. These women reported more problems and more *serious* problems than persons of all other classes. They reported more disagreements, less functional methods of conflict resolution, and, perhaps as importantly, fewer compensatory rewards in their lives. Financial insecurity, unpleasant neighborhoods, and child- rearing difficulties were concurrent stressors which contributed to exacerbate marital problems. All in all, it is not unfair to say that, *on the average, when a lower-class woman divorces, she has suffered a great deal more than other women who divorce.* And their children suffer more than privileged children.

THE COUPLE PERSPECTIVE ON HAPPINESS

I was especially interested in examining marital happiness and perceptions within each ex-dyad. In Table VI.3, of the 84 *couples* for whom the data were available for both ex-spouses, only 19% reported a similar level of past marital happiness. All other ex-couples reported different levels of past marital happiness. However, when there was a difference within an ex-pair, the difference tended to be of one degree only. Only 6% of the ex-pairs had a difference of 3, which would indicate that, in such ex-pairs, one ex-spouse had been happy while the other had been unhappy. Later on, we will present cases of ex-dyads who had a large difference and compare them with those who had a similar feeling about their past marital happiness.

Spouses currently married to each other tended to be much more congruent in assessing their own marital happiness: 58% gave the same answer. Moreover, not one of the 101 couples gave an answer which indicated a wide discrepancy in marital happiness. Two explanations can be offered for this difference in congruence between couples and ex-couples. First, marriages that end in divorce are more likely to include spouses who have a different level of marital happiness. Such a discrepancy would contribute to an imbalance in the marriage and the imbalance would be more keenly felt by the less advantaged spouse (generally the woman, as women had lower levels of happiness than men). Second, although not mutually exclusive, the explanation could be that post-divorce conditions contribute to differences in recall or, still, time alone creates a "faulty" memory.

The first explanation was borne out of the data. The second explanation is erroneous *in this sample* because both men and women were very stable over time in their evaluation of their past marriage: persons interviewed two or three times tended to give the same score each time even though two and three years had elapsed between the interviews and even though they were asked over two hundred questions by 1984.

Table IV.3. Dyadic Congruence of Marital Happiness in Current and Previous Marriages
(in percent)

	No Difference Between Spouses	1-point Difference	2-point Difference	3-point Difference
Current Marriages	58	34	9	0
Past Marriages	19	45	30	6

Correlations Between Spouses', As Well As Between Ex-Spouses', Actual Marital Happiness

Ex-Spouses' Score Correlations on Reported Past Happiness $r = .2635, p < .008, N = 84$	Spouses' Score Correlations on Reported Marital Happiness $r = .6296, p < .000, N = 101$

Another way of looking at the level of agreement within each couple is presented in the lower panel of Table IV.3. On the left-hand side, we see that ex-spouses had a comparatively low correlation, although still highly significant. What is of greater relevance here is the comparative size of the correlations between ex-couples and current couples. Spouses married to each other reached a correlation of .6296 in terms of their reported marital happiness.

In order further to study the level of marital happiness at the couple level, I devised a composite score for each couple by totalling the scores of both ex-spouses and did the same for both spouses. Had I opted to derive an average, the dyads with differences of 2 or 3 between the spouses would have biased the results. I obtained three categories of dyads from the totals. First, a dyad would have a high level of marital happiness with totals of 2, 3, or 4. These scores mean that both spouses or ex-spouses had had a very high marital happiness. A dyadic score of 4 could be obtained if both spouses reported a fairly high level of marital happiness or one had an average happiness while the other was very happy. Mid-level dyads were those with scores of 5, 6, 7 and low-level dyads had scores of 8, 9, 10. Their marital happiness was very low, hence the term "low-level" dyads. In Table IV.4, we see that 13% (or 11) of the ex-dyads had a high level of past marital

Table VI.4. Dyadic Levels of Marital Happiness in Current
and Previous Marriages
(in percent)

	High-level Dyads (scores of 2,3,4)	Mid-level Dyads (scores of 5,6,7)	Low-level Dyads (scores of 8,9,10)
Current marriages	79	21	2
Past Marriages	13	52	34.5

happiness. A majority of the ex-dyads (52%) were mid level (total scores of 5, 6 or 7) and 34.5% were at a low level of marital happiness.

In contrast, as would be expected by the individual scores seen in Tables IV.1 and IV.2, a majority of the currently married couples were at a high level of marital happiness and only two were at a low level. Again these data indicate that recently married couples are likely to be high-level couples in terms of marital happiness. Although we know from other studies that *individual* marital happiness declines over the years to be revitalized at retirement, we do not know how the *couple* level fluctuates over time or over the life span. This, I hope, other researchers will follow-up.

EX-COUPLES: CASE STUDIES

In this chapter, as in the previous one, case studies are presented to allow us a more detailed profile of various types of couples and ex-couples in terms of marital happiness—past and present. The first case vignette to be presented is that of an ex-couple who reported a high level of past marital happiness.

Linda Marshall is a 32-year-old Ph.D. student, still unremarried; Jonathan Marshall, her 34-year-old ex-husband, is remarried to a 26-year-old woman who has a two-year-old girl from her previous marriage. Jonathan is a professional and has remarried a year ago. He and Linda have not maintained any relationship and would not care to. He reported his past marriage as having been very happy and she reported it as fairly happy. (In all three cases of a dyadic score of 3, the ex-husband reported a very happy past marriage.) Jonathan also rates his current marriage as very happy.

Jonathan and Linda had been married for four years during which time she was unfaithful to him and ended up leaving him for another man rather abruptly. Jonathan was "too bland" for her and she had "fallen in love" with this man whom she later left for still another man; the latter supported her through her doctoral studies, while she was being unfaithful to him as well. Linda felt she was to blame for the demise of her marriage because of a sudden change in her ideals and goals. She had, however, no regrets and no guilt feelings. She mentioned being a feminist but was rather utilitarian about it: "I can't say I like the company of women. But I can use the ideology." She gave the impression of a woman spoiled by men. Jonathan blamed her for the divorce and had harbored strong regrets for two years. He compared his current wife to Linda thusly: "She is less sophisticated and independent and more home oriented and wants a larger family. I have more time to devote to my career. My wife is not the liberated type and I come first and it's nice for a change."

At a somewhat lower level on the SES scale, we have another ex-couple with a high dyadic marital satisfaction and congruence: both rated their past marriage as fairly happy. This ex-couple is also described in the previous chapter. Ray Dodge is a 44-year-old unremarried telephone installation supervisor and his ex-wife, Diana Martin, is remarried to a small businessman whom she helps. Ray and Diana were married for 16 years, have two married children, both in their twenties, and one grandchild.

Neither blames the other for the divorce. Ray: "We just grew apart and no longer wanted the same things out of life." Diana added to this: "he could have been home more, but at least he was not cheating out on me." He admits to being "beer and car crazy." He has no regrets: "It all turned out fine, I do what I want and she's got what she wants." Diana expressed some regrets at Time 2: "I was sorry because we got along pretty well." But her regrets were not "very serious." Before terminating their marriage they had both discussed their planned separation and divorce and decided upon it together.

Unlike the previous ex-couple, Ray and Diana see each other every other month because of their children, grandchild, "and the other grandchild on the way." They described each other in cordial terms. They were one of the few ex-couples in the study whose conversations with each other went beyond their children: "I ask him about his cars and he asks me about my husband and the business. It's somewhat like talking to my cousin."

These two vignettes of ex-dyads with a high level of past marital happiness well illustrate the dilemma of trying to establish generalizations. Perhaps the one link between these past marriages is that one of the two spouses in each marriage had interests, activities or hobbies which kept him or her from investing into the marriage. While the marriage lasts, the externally-invested spouse is happy—busy as he or she is elsewhere—and the more marriage-oriented spouse begins to suffer; but the marriage breaks down *before* animosity or all-out warfare erupts. Thus, both ex-spouses have experienced a marriage which was very or fairly happy, or reconstruct it as such. However, as indicated earlier, longitudinal respondents were asked about their past marital happiness three times: their answers were very consistent over time. This leads to the conclusion that the marriage was indeed relatively happy and that there is no retrospective bias.

The attention is now turned to cases of wide discrepancy in marital happiness and, later, to ex-dyads with a low level of past marital happiness. There were five ex-dyads where the ex-spouses had a discrepancy of 3; in two cases, the ex-husbands had been very to fairly happy and in three it had been the ex-wives who had been very to fairly happy, the other spouse having been unhappy.

Bruno Matieri is a 35-year-old construction supervisor of Italian background who was staying with a married sister in 1984. He had an 8-year-old daughter living with his ex-wife, Mary, who had remarried three years earlier. Mary also has a 1-year-old son from her remarriage. Their marriage had lasted six years and Bruno rated it as fairly happy. Mary, currently a housekeeper and formerly a school teacher, is English Canadian. She considers herself very religious (Catholic). She rated her first marriage as very unhappy. Bruno and Mary see each other every other week but she longs for the time her daughter will be old enough so that she, Mary, will not have to see her ex-husband. Mary: "We talk about visits and that's it. Now he's become more polite and asks me how I am but he ignores my son. A son is very important for an Italian man and he doesn't have one, and I am certain he is very jealous."

She describes Bruno as domineering and old-fashioned. He admitted to having had affairs while married and pointed out that he and his ex-wife were sexually "incompatible." "I threatened to leave if he didn't stop seeing other women. I put up with it for two years, that I knew of, and then I sued him for divorce." Her two marriages are not comparable: "The two men are complete opposites. To this day, I feel I was very immature and naive to have married my former husband because he had quite a reputation. I guess I have no one to blame but myself."

Bruno intends to remarry one day. It will be to an Italian woman, preferably one from his parents' village, younger in order to start a new family: "Canadian women are too spoiled. They don't look after their men properly and they always complain." He intends to have four or five more children and when this occurs he foresees that his daughter will become less important to him; he resents the role her stepfather plays in her life.

In the following vignette of two ex-spouses with a large discrepancy, it is the ex-wife who had had a fairly happy marriage and the ex-husband a very unhappy one. Ben Klein, age 40, owns a fairly substantial business and is remarried to another business woman his age. He has three live-in stepchildren while his own two daughters live with Rhoda, his ex-wife. She is age 33 and also remarried. Both Ben and Rhoda remarried within their Jewish faith. Ben attributes the demise of their 14-year marriage to her emotional problems: "I felt smothered, I was choking under the weight of the responsibilities she was constantly heaping upon me. She's a good woman but she is so terribly dependent you have no idea how it is. ... I love having children and at first enjoyed having a child-wife but when the children came and started growing up, I couldn't take the burden. We moved from Montreal and suddenly she was left without [her family] and she just couldn't cope."

Unfortunately for him, his ex-wife remarried a man "who is more than useless. He drinks more than is good for him and gives her no moral support. He makes a living and he's found a woman who jumps when he says jump." Ben is very concerned about his daughters: "Yes, I feel pulled because my wife and I have two alcoholics on our hands so to speak although her ex-husband is basically a good man."

Rhoda corroborates her former husband's impressions, although from a different perspective. She attributed her divorce to her dependency and his boredom with it all. She also admitted still depending on Ben. She showed a great deal of personal insight but did not let on that she could think for herself. She sees a psychiatrist.

No, I don't think my husband would want me to see a woman psychiatrist. My husband thinks a woman's place is at home. So do I. A woman psychiatrist might tell me to go to work and I couldn't cope with that. This is not what I need. I am a quiet, loving person.

Aren't you afraid *I* might tell you to go to work?

Well, I wouldn't have to do it ... I've never told anyone before that *I don't* think I have a psychiatric problem. If I disagree with this, my doctor won't see me and my husband will not like it. I use the psychiatrist to pacify everyone. So long as I am *really* helpless, they'll help me but if I were not helpless, my former husband might not help me so much and my husband would be threatened. You may think I am paranoid.

[silence]

No? [Laughs] You agree?

Makes sense.

Well, I'll think about that some more when you're gone.

In the above two vignettes, one ex-spouse had been quite content with the way things had been going for him or her in the previous marriage. That spouse was having his or her own way to the detriment of the other. The marriages had also lasted long enough to produce children and unhappiness in the other ex-spouse. These were cases of imbalance: different perceptions of what a marriage ought to be, clashing personality types, even parasitic relationships. The suffering spouses (Mary in one marriage and Ben in the other) had tried very hard to accommodate but could no longer cope with the suppression of their own needs and even personalities. Moreover,the problems experienced in the previous marriages had a carry over into the remarriages; the burden was not entirely eradicated by the divorce as a relationship had to be maintained because of the children.

The next vignette is that of a dyad with a very high level of past marital unhappiness; both ex-spouses had been very unhappy.

Janice Smith is a 43-year-old welfare mother of 5 children (and 3 grandchildren). In 1984, only two of these children were still living at home with her. She had been separated/divorced from Joe Smith for 11 years. He is a 44-year-old unemployed laborer and has been living common-law with his fourth wife for two years, although technically he is still only separated from his third wife. Both ex-spouses are Protestant.

Eleven years ago, Joe decided to leave his wife of 15 years. He mentioned he might leave and, one day, he did. She described the causes leading to their divorce as: his infidelity, drinking, cruelty, financial problems, sexual incompatibility and "we never loved each other anyway." But, she added: "I am responsible because I married him and I knew from the beginning that I would be unhappy." She had no employment history, was on welfare most of her married life and has so been since her separation.

Joe mentioned his own boredom, financial problems, sexual incompatibility, his own falling out of love, and the fact that they did not get along as the chief causes of his divorce from Janice. However, he mentioned these exact same causes for his other two divorces as well. He had been employed off and on all his adult life and, a long-time alcoholic, was still drinking by 1984. Besides his five children from Janice, he had two other children from his second ex-wife who also ended up on welfare and got off it only when she remarried. His three ex-wives reported a very similar marital experience with him: a life of misery, abuse, alcohol, and nonsupport. Both Joe and Janice came from families with a history of poverty, deprivation, and parental separation.

The ex-dyads with low levels of past marital happiness had had stormy marriages with a great deal of discord. Alcoholism, wife battering, unemployment were trademarks, and the ex-spouses were more likely to be found at the lower than the higher end of the SES scale. These ex-dyads were also characterized by poor relationships after the separation, and desertion had been a common means of ending the marriage. In other words, ex-dyads with low levels of past marital happiness fell more clearly into categories than did ex-dyads at mid level or even high level of past marital happiness. They tended to be "typical" cases of divorce involving what we expect a poor marriage to be. However, the other types of dyads were not so easily categorizable.

REMARRIED COUPLES: CASE STUDIES

The first vignette of remarried couples is that of a high-level dyad in terms of marital happiness. Because 79% of the couples were at this level, it was not possible to find one that was necessarily representative of the others. As we will see later, unhappy couples and couples with a discrepancy between the spouses are easier to categorize, as was the case in terms of divorce. Nevertheless, as we read about the four couples introduced, we will easily notice a deterioration in the quality of the marital relationship as we pass from high to mid to low levels of marital happiness.

Jim and May Kerr, remarried for four years after a one and a half year courtship, have twin boy/girl age 3. Jim also has a 14-year-old son; the son lives with his own mother/stepfather. May had two sons from her previous marriage and they have always been in their father's custody. They are age 17 and age 13.

While Jim's relationship with his ex-wife and her husband is very cordial, May's relationship with her ex-husband is unpleasant. He has alternated between being irritated by her attempts to gain more liberal access to her sons and then accusing her of not seeing them enough, especially after the birth of the twins. It was obvious in his interviews that he had used their sons against her. In contrast, Jim had a good relationship with his son and the stepfather was very cooperative. May's parents even include Jim's son in their outings with the twins when Jim's son is visiting. The boy is very attached to his young twin half siblings. He occasionally sees May's sons but does not get along with them so well as the latter two are relatively difficult. May's sons definitely are ambivalent about their twin half siblings.

Jim's relationship with his stepsons is "not too close" although he would prefer to see them more often—perhaps for his wife's sake. He does believe, however, that he would be happier without these stepsons, although he also believes that they create no problem in his relationship with his wife. May's relationship with her stepson is "as close as it can be without being detrimental to the relationship with his mother." He is attached to her and feels that her own sons should visit her more often.

This combination of half siblings and step-children with varying levels of attachment to one another could be problematic for the remarriage, but May and Jim have integrated the stepchildren into their new lives, albeit only to the extent that these adolescents are willing to be cooperative. At the very least, the stepchildren do not detract from the marriage as was frequently the case in other remarriages in the sample (see chapter on stepparenting).

May, age 39, occupies a supervisory position in a large department store. She completed a M.B.A. after her separation. She and Jim employ a full-time housekeeper. May describes her current marriage as: "I am a partner ... in many ways including our mutual stepchildren and management of ex-spouses. We always stand by each other. We're together but we are individuals as well; we have our own areas of directorship, if you wish. He doesn't tell me what to do about my sons and vice versa or about my parents and vice versa. He shares in the upbringing of our children whereas I had to do it all in my previous marriage. He is thoughtful and we plan everything together. In my first marriage, it was all *his* life; his home was his castle. I was a fringe benefit."

Jim, age 43, has a mid-level executive position and graduate school. He felt he had outgrown his ex-wife whereas, "in this marriage, we are always ahead of each other and learning from each other. I love to love my wife because I know she could have any other man [she is a very attractive woman] or she could do without me. She does not need a man but she needs me and it's great."

Gender equality is certainly a theme that runs through this marriage and gratifies both partners. It is, in fact, a theme which I frequently encountered: either in comparison to a less equal previous marriage, as in the Kerr case, or as something which is lacking in the marriage. In the latter instance, it was often encountered in couples which were composed of a man remarried to a much younger woman who had been previously single. These younger women were particularly dissatisfied, except in instances of great upward mobility of the much younger and much less educated woman (see the chapter on age differences).

However, the sample also included several couples high in marital happiness for whom gender *inequality*, and complementarity of functions, formed one of the cornerstones of their happiness. Although these tended to be couples in which the wife was older than age 45, younger couples also fell in this category. At this point in time, it does appear that gender equality as a source of marital happiness fits better within a high education and career orientation context. In this sample, less educated and less achievement oriented women were not so likely to need gender equality as a cornerstone of marital happiness.

The next vignette is that of a mid-level couple where the spouses are not congruent. The 40-year-old wife, a daycare worker, is rather dissatisfied with her husband and scored 4 out of a low 5 on marital happiness: "somewhat unhappy." Her husband, a 43-year-old unemployed accountant, scored a relatively high 2 or "fairly happy." "I'd be happier if I had a steady job. I'd like to be able to say that I support my wife, and I don't like being the one who does the housework."

Ron and Kim Moore have been married for two years following a 6- to 8-month courtship. Both are Protestant. Ron had no children and his first ex-wife lives in the United States. His second ex-wife has remarried and is a housewife with an infant and a toddler. He has no relationship with either ex-wives. Kim is his third wife. While he believes there is a 90% chance of still being with Kim in 10 years, she gives it a 50-75% chance.

Kim's divorce (and remarriage) has meant considerable downward social mobility for her as her former husband is a lawyer who remarried an advertising executive. She regrets her first marriage and the lifestyle she had. Kim has four children from that marriage: the two girls age 10 and 8 are in her custody while the boys age 15 and 17 are in his custody. She has a good relationship with her former spouse and his new wife. She initially had had the custody of all children but her ex-husband requested the sons after her remarriage. She stresses that their father makes certain that her sons maintain a good relationship with her and are dutiful toward her.

Kim describes herself as a person who has always been weak and insecure, traits which "tired out" her former husband. She sees herself as "everyone's child"—her parents', her former husband's, and her psychiatrist's. Her current husband "argues more, he is less secure, less in control, in a way he is like me and that's not too good for either of us." She adds, "I wanted to remarry because I can't live by myself." (She is to be contrasted with May Kerr who waited longer between marriages as she was independent.) "I need support but my husband is not very supportive. He has his problems and he is unemployed most of the time. So what I got really, was another person to take care of, it's as if I had traded my sons for another son, except that this one doesn't have a father to help me out with him."

She also explained that, had she remained single, her former husband would have supported her entirely financially and "I would not have to work, I work so hard [daycare], I do a young woman's job." Also, her sons would come "more often, so I don't think I did such a good thing by getting married." For his part, Ron suffers in his own comparison of himself with Kim's former husband. "He thinks his children should have a better stepfather ... My wife had to get work last year because he doesn't pay enough for his daughters' support and he told her, of all things, that he didn't want to contribute to *my* living."

Ron is fairly satisfied with his wife and much prefers her to his previous one. He finds her reasonable, not "complaining like the other did," and easy to get along with. He is not too fond of his stepchildren but acknowledges that the little girls are "easy like their mother." The girls also explain their financial security in spite of his unemployment because Kim's ex-husband has left her the house until the girls move out. Ron appreciates this aspect of having the two little girls with them. He added at some point that his wife gets along with her parents who, in both persons' opinion, meddle. "Maybe she should stand up for herself but if she did she might be difficult for me to handle as well and I've got enough problems without having a difficult wife."

Neither spouse is particularly attractive physically; they are more on the average side. Ron's personality had definitely improved since his first interview and even Kim acknowledged that he was doing much better since they had married. Kim, although definitely insecure, is certainly not as dependent and immature as her family and her ex-husband see her. The house was well kept, the two little girls were well behaved, neat, talkative, normal; she held a hard job and her husband had definitely improved since I first met him. Neither spouse is completely certain of the stability of their marriage and Kim definitely suffers from relative deprivation, given her past. It is difficult to predict the long-term stability of this marriage as Ron has a history of multiple divorces and Kim may "grow up" one day and leave.

The next two cases are of low-level happiness couples. The first one consists of a 31-year-old wife, hostess at a restaurant, who also does typing on the side. Nina has custody of her 12-year-old daughter. She was previously married to a Catholic Lebanese, owner of a small business. Nina has been married to Roger Thompson for two years after a 15-month courtship. Roger is a 30-year-old restaurant chef whose four children (three girls age 9, 8, 6 and a 4-year-old boy) live with their remarried mother, a stripper, whose husband operates a snow removal/landscape outfit.

Nina rated herself as somewhat unhappy, or 4 out of a low 5 while Roger rated himself "neither happy nor unhappy" or 3. While Roger gave a 50% chance to their marriage survival, Nina gave it a zero chance! Nina: "Right now, I suspect we will leave each other within a year or so and it doesn't even upset me anymore. I know I can take care of myself and my daughter. Her father pays for her now and I always get a better job each year. I am still young and I might even get remarried but I can see myself living alone with my daughter. If that's all there is to marriage, it's not worth it."

What are her sources of dissatisfaction? First, she suspects that Roger is seeing other women. She is quite right, as Roger confirmed his dalliances during his interview. Second, Roger's four children are a burden to her as they visit at least twice a month. Her daughter has to help her care for them and her own parents even have to pitch in. "The boy is spoiled and is not well disciplined." However, Roger prefers the boy over the nicer girls. Moreover, Nina knows that Roger does not give enough for the support of his children and his ex-wife has to come to her to get money. She sympathizes with the ex-wife and her difficult job as an "exotic dancer" or stripper.

For his part, Roger does not think that going out with his wife helps their relationship and they consequently share few activities. He finds Nina suspicious. Nevertheless, for the time being, even if his wife found out about his womanizing, he would want to stay with her: "She's easy to live with. She pulls her weight and the father gives money for the girl, so we are alright. With another woman [a new wife] I might have to support her and her kids and I have mine; I can't stand to think about it. I am not saying that this is the greatest family on earth but right now it's fine by me."

The next couple, Matthew and Lucille Walker, have been remarried for four years. Matthew, age 33, is a professional, albeit not a hugely successful one, while Lucille, age 28, is a photographer. He is of Catholic background and she of

Protestant. There were no children from their previous marriages and there are no children of this union. Linda wants children, "but not in this marriage." Matthew does not want any. They had dated for five months before marrying. They both had been separated for two years.

Lucille rated her marriage as very unhappy or 5, and Matthew rated it as somewhat unhappy at 4. Thus, this is a very low-level couple in terms of marital happiness. She gives no chance of survival to her marriage while he gives it a 40% chance. Says he, "The way it's going, I am surprised we have gone this far. Her family and friends talk about my drinking. I admit, I like drinking but it is not really a problem because I bother no one and I don't even go out on her. So I avoid her family and friends and this means we don't do too much together." He has a practical point of view: "This marriage is just [as unsatisfactory] as the other one. So long as they [marriages] are all the same, I just do not see the point in divorcing again and getting married and so on. It may not be a good marriage but I don't see too many good marriages around and I don't feel too bad about it. I certainly am not a minority."

Matthew was clinically depressed at interview time. His speech was slow and he searched for his words. He was taking psychotropic drugs. He had two drinks during the session, and left for more once his interview was completed. Lucille looked tired and drawn. She had deep circles beneath the eyes and was too thin. She pointed out that Matthew should be seeing his psychiatrist more often.

Lucille's first marriage had not been very happy "but there were very good points in it." It ended when she walked in on her husband while he was having sexual intercourse with his little daughter from a previous marriage. Lucille: "He is hard to get along with; he doesn't care about anything except drinking. He is inoffensive but he is a wreck." However, she is not yet ready to face another divorce "although my friends tell me I should leave because I am young and I surely can meet a nice man." Her reason to leave will eventually be her desire for a child. "Right now, I have quite a bit of money set aside but there are advantages to this marriage. I get to go out with my friends and do things I really like to do. Maybe what I should do is just have an affair with a nice man and have a child. Then I might have the courage to leave."

OVERVIEW

Marriages that were relatively happy and ended up in a divorce are difficult to categorize in terms of a common thread. They, however, generally consisted of one spouse who was less happy in the marriage than the other. In other instances, one spouse had outside interests that were not or could not be shared by the other. In both cases, there was an imbalance in satisfaction and/or investment in the marriage and this imbalance ultimately led to divorce. Such couples generally maintain a good relationship with each other after separation when they have children. These marriages are devoid of open conflict and the decision to divorce is generally reached amicably (see Chapter III).

There were happy marriages that ended because of "accidents." That is, the divorce was brought about following the discovery by one spouse of the other's sexual indiscretions. I call these indiscretions "accidental" because they were not planned and generally happened during business trips, office parties, and other occasions excluding the other spouse. The unfaithful spouse had no intention of pursuing the indiscretion. Nevertheless, "bad habits" are sometimes formed and the irresponsible attitude becomes a marital risk. Such persons have been too complacent about their marriage. I would call this "taking risks with one's marriage." Often, the offending party is more upset by the breakup than the offended spouse. Generally, however, post- separation relationships are reasonable in contrast to marriages that ended after one of the spouses had had a real affair or had developed an attachment to a third party. These divorces were full of acrimony and the cheated party, usually the wife, felt devalued.

As a general rule, happy marriages that end in divorce represent what could be called "useless divorces." These are divorces which could have been easily prevented. The pain caused by the consequences is not worth it as it may be in the case of couples who divorce after a very bad marriage. Often, one or both spouses remarry someone similar to the previous spouse and, as one man put it: "I just traded one perfectly good wife for another perfectly good wife. You sort of wonder what the point of it all is."

Couples who were happily remarried also defied generalizations after an average of only 2.8 years of remarriage. However, one theme was common: the remarriage provides both with something important which had been lacking in their previous marriage or had made them miserable (with the exception of the "accidents" previously described—even here, the new spouses want to make sure that such accidents will not be repeated). Large age differences were generally, but not always, excluded from happy remarriages. As well, the good of the stepchildren was often secondary to the good of the new union. Actually, when live-out stepchildren were given too much importance by one of the two spouses, the remarriage generally suffered. Children from a previous marriage are, to be cynical but realistic, the price that remarriages have to pay—at times with disastrous consequences.

Unhappy remarriages, like unhappy marriages which had ended in divorce, were more easily categorizable. There were already, after only 2.8 years of marriage, deep dissatisfactions with the partner, points of contention (unemployment, alcoholism, stepchildren, future goals), adultery, and a feeling of precariousness or of relationship instability. (The remarriages included in this chapter were the ones that had already survived the initial remarriage period.) Unhappy remarriages were characterized as well by a briefer courtship period and either a very satisfying previous marriage or another previous marriage that had been unhappy.

NOTE

1. It is not the purpose of this chapter to present a thorough overview of marital *satisfaction*, adjustment or the quality of marital life in general. See studies such as those by Norton (1983), Spanier (1976, 1979), Spanier and Lewis (1980), and Spanier et al. (1979).

Chapter V

Multiply-Divorced Persons and Their Ex-Spouses:
A Comparison with the Once-Divorced

Women expect too much of marriage. I sure as hell can't live out their dreams.

—Man in his fourth marriage

I can't live alone. I need a man but I can't say I have much choice as to who I marry. I close my eyes and hope it'll turn out alright.

—Woman divorced twice

My wife says I have to work at our marriage. I don't agree with her. Marriage is supposed to be pleasant and if it isn't, well, it's not my problem.

—Man in his third marriage

All my four wives are different from each other. The first was into getting married, having money, turning me into a good Jewish husband; the second wanted a child but was nice and sweet and easy; the third was calculating, organized, and cool and had a mind, and my wife is, well she's an actress, she's dramatic, she lives life like it's a TV drama, she's restless, always into something new, fashionable, expensive. She's like me and likes excitement.

—Man in his fourth marriage.

The literature on divorce has increased substantially within the past five years in response to social trends and the demand for information from the public. Yet, because of the recency of this research explosion, review articles and books indicate how little is still known about marital dissolution by separation or divorce (Goetting 1981; Kitson and Raschke 1981; Levinger and Moles 1979). One of the gaps concerns persons who go through multiple divorces. Research on redivorce is so rare that a 1981 review article on that topic could only discuss the rate of divorce among people who remarry following a divorce (Day and MacKey 1981). A book by Fox (1983), based on a sample of 18 respondents, is the only lengthy exploration of this topic. An article by Counts and Reid (1987) presents a clinical typology of the multiply-divorced. A second gap in the literature on divorce in general is that, as is the case for research on the family, the couple perspective is lacking. Accordingly, to this date, there is no published research that has studied persons with multiple divorces along with their ex-spouses.

Therefore, the research reported in this chapter is a first step in studying multiple divorces beyond the demographic perspective. It should be added that the incidence of multiple divorce is relatively low and it is unavoidable that only a fraction of my original sample had been divorced more than once as I did not have the material resources to over-sample for multiple divorces. Indeed, only 19 of the 208 divorced and formerly-divorced respondents had been multiply-divorced: 3 had been divorced three times, and 16 had been divorced twice. In 1984, 13 of the 19 multiply-divorced were remarried. Whenever possible, all the ex-spouses as well as the current spouse of the multiply-divorced were interviewed.

In the first two sections, the multiply-divorced will be compared to the once-divorced. In our society, multiple divorces are both a statistical and a normative deviance, while single divorces have become more acceptable. Therefore, people who divorce repeatedly can logically be expected to be different on certain dimensions. In other words, is there a selection process leading to multiple divorces? Another section will ask: Do particular persons tend to marry higher-risk spouses? Or, are the multiply-divorced victims of a particular type of spouses they tend to choose? If this were the case, one should expect that the ex-spouses of the multiply-divorced would be substantially different from the ex-spouses of the once-divorced. The next section asks: Will a person tend repeatedly to marry spouses who are similar to each other? For instance, if the multiply-divorced repeatedly were to remarry high-risk persons who resemble each other, this might explain their recurring divorces

The last two sections will first turn to the ex-spouses within each set to see how they perceive the one spouse they have shared serially. Such data might indicate whether the multiply-divorced tended to be constant in their behavior throughout their various marriages or if they adapted to the different persons they married (assuming such persons were different—this question is also studied). The focus will be more specifically on the perceived causes of divorce within each set of ex-spouses. I wanted to know how the multiply-divorced perceived their various marital breakups and whether their perception matched that of their ex-spouses.

DEMOGRAPHIC CHARACTERISTICS

On the average the multiply-divorced were 40-years-old while the once-divorced were age 38. Thus, differences between the two groups cannot be explained by age. (There was no difference in age between respondents who had divorced twice and those who had divorced thrice.) They had begun their marital careers only six months earlier than the once-divorced, at age 21; the first marriage had lasted equally long, nearly 10 years, while second and third marriages became briefer (2.3 years and one year respectively) (Norton 1983). Separations between recouplings were shorter than was the case for the once-divorced (2.3 years vs. 3.3 years), and so was the dating period preceding a new union: 71% dated their current spouse less than nine months while only 38% of the once-divorced dated so briefly before remarrying or living together.

Whereas once-divorced persons had 1.6 children from their previous marriage, the multiply-divorced had 2.2, generally from one marriage only—the reverse occurred in Fox's (1983) study. This discrepancy between the two studies stems from the fact that, at Time 1 of the longitudinal research, emphasis had been placed on locating divorced persons with children because children's behavior was a topic of interest at that stage of the study. Therefore, the multiply-divorced in our sample were more likely than those in another sample to have had children and to have had a longer first marriage.

I found, as Fox did, the multiply-divorced to have a lower education level, although none of the tests approached significance level. For instance, 45% had no more than a high school diploma, but only 28% of the once-divorced had so little education. Yearly personal income tended to be lower for the multiply-divorced, but, once again, the tests were not significant. When considering overall socioeconomic status on a 7-point scale (1 = highest SES), the multiply-divorced averaged 5 and the once-divorced 4.1 ($p < .021$). The lower socioeconomic status among the multiply-divorced does not, however, explain the differences to be reported between them and the once-divorced: once I controlled for SES, the differences between the multiply and the once-divorced presented in the following sections remained. Therefore, while a disproportionate number of the multiply-divorced were of lower SES, this lower status in itself probably did not account for their propensity to multiple divorce. As indicated below, the answer lies more with their familial background, their own psychological assets, as well as certain "chance" or risk factors, such as marrying other multiply-divorced persons.

THE MULTIPLY-DIVORCED
VERSUS THE ONCE-DIVORCED

In Table V.1, data are presented comparing the once-divorced to the multiply-divorced on a number of key variables. An abbreviation of the wording of the questions asked is presented, and each question is numbered for subsequent referral in the text. When appropriate, *t* tests were also performed: all were significant when the chi-squares were. A chi-square presentation was chosen because it suited all data gathered whereas only certain questions could be analyzed via t tests.

There is some modest evidence in the literature for the transmission of marital instability across generations (Bumpass and Sweet 1972; Glenn and Kramer 1987; Mueller and Pope 1977). It is seen in Table V.1, that the multiply-divorced came from a broken home more often than the once-divorced, and more did not know their father's current whereabouts. Perhaps related to this

Table V.1. Percentage Comparisons Between
the Multiply-divorced and the Once-divorced

	Once-divorced (%)	Multiply-divorced (%)	Chi-square	df	p
1. Parents still living together	82.8	64.7	7.13	2	.032
2. Know where father lives	97.0	84.0	6.22	2	.043
3. Happy during adolescence	51.0	11.0	19.06	4	.000
4. Father lives within 100 mile radius	49.5	31.6	10.56	6	.103
5. Mother lives within 100 mile radius	56.8	42.0	6.73	6	.346
6. Talked to parents over phone past week	49.5	29.4	1.76	1	.184
7. Visited parents past month	53.8	35.3	1.47	1	.226
8. Occasionally turned to parents for help	38.8	11.8	3.81	1	.051
9. Talked with sibling over phone past week	47.0	17.6	4.37	1	.036
10. Visited a sibling past month	60.0	41.0	1.57	1	.210
11. First marriage very unhappy	41.7	66.6	9.93	5	.077
12. Friendly relationship with first ex-spouse	22.5	5.6	11.71	5	.037
13. See first ex-spouse at least once a month	33.4	16.7	10.72	4	.038
14. High likelihood still be with current spouse in 10 years	86.9	61.6	24.15	6	.005
15. Turn to spouse when help needed	62.0	33.0	3.59	1	.057
16. Close relationship with children from previous marriage	78.8	42.8	22.28	8	.004
17. See children at least once a month	75.3	45.5	9.52	2	.019
18. Talk with children over the phone at least once a month	90.6	63.6	9.75	2	.007
19. Overall health self-rated as good	87.3	77.8	18.34	4	.001
20. Had *not* felt an impending nervous breakdown past year	84.7	55.6	7.60	1	.005
21. Rarely/never feel tense	69.9	44.5	6.12	3	.105
22. Feel have a lot of control over life	31.7	11.1	9.52	4	.049
23. Rarely/never feel down/low	78.2	44.4	12.57	3	.005
24. *No* psychothropic drugs past two weeks	58.7	22.2	9.53	2	.008
25. Had consumed 4 + drinks at one sitting	6.9	22.2	11.78	5	.038
26. *Not* treated for emotional problems past year	87.8	57.9	9.86	1	.001

(continued on next page)

Table V.1. (continued)

	Once-divorced (%)	Multiply-divorced (%)	Chi-square	df	p
27. *Not* treated for emotional problems after first marriage	72.6	43.8	4.53	1	.033
28. *Not* treated for emotional problems during current marriage	96.0	56.0	9.89	1	.001
29. For help turn to professionals	23.3	55.6	7.28	1	.007

was the fact that a greater proportion of the multiply-divorced described themselves as having been unhappy during adolescence: 78% versus 28%. Thus, they came from a family background shrouded in greater instability and unhappiness; *the theory of the transmission of marital instability across generations may be particularly applicable to the multiply-divorced.*

Not only did the multiply-divorced stem from a more unstable family background, but they were also less close to their parents and siblings at the time of the 1984 interview. They were less close geographically, and were less close to their parents on the following indicators: fewer had talked to parents over the phone in the past week, fewer had visited with their parents during the past month, and relatively few turned to parents for help. Moreover, although the multiply-divorced had a larger sib group (3.1 vs. 2.5 siblings), they were less close socially to their siblings than were the once-divorced as indicated in Table V.1 by item 9.

In the area of marital life, their current relationship with their first ex-spouse was less good than that of the once-divorced. It was less friendly, more filled with dislike, and angrier. Whereas 23% of the once-divorced reported a warm and friendly relationship with their ex-spouses, only 6% of the multiply-divorced did. It should be noted that their relationships with second and third ex-spouses were no better. In terms of contact, only 17% saw their first ex-spouse once a month or more, while 33% of the once-divorced did—this in spite of the fact that the multiply-divorced had more children from that ex-spouse. Neither did they compensate by seeing their second or third ex-spouses: only three ever saw their other ex-spouses and two of these had been married to each other at some point. Phone conversations followed the same pattern.

The multiply-divorced had a tendency to marry, at some point in their marital career, another person who was also multiply-divorced; 42% did so while only 16% of the once-divorced had done so. This marital homogamy may compound the risk of divorce among these respondents as they marry other "risky" persons. (However, as will be shown later, this is actually the only instance of "risk" that was found among the ex-spouses.) As indicated by item 14, the thirteen respondents who were married for a third or fourth time during the field work were much less optimistic about being still married to that same person in ten years. They also reported turning to their current spouse less often than did the remarried once-divorced (33% versus 62%—item 15), one more indicator of the probably greater fragility of their current remarriage or, at the very least, their lesser involvement in that relationship than was generally the case for the remarried once-divorced.

In terms of parental role, once again there was a sharp contrast between the two categories; a majority of the once-divorced who had children from a previous marriage reported a very or fairly close relationship with their children (75%), but only a third of the multiply-divorced so qualified their relationship. A majority of the multiply-divorced were non-custodial parents. When children did not live with them, the once-divorced reported seeing their children and talking to them over the phone at least once a month more often than the multiply-divorced (items 17 and 18). Thus, the latter did not fulfill their coparental role to the same extent that the once-divorced did. Their ex-spouses confirmed these results as they tended to describe their multiply-divorced ex-spouses in terms indicating that they were not adequate parents and were, even, poor role models for their children.

So far, we have seen that the multiply-divorced were more isolated from their parents, siblings, ex-spouses, and children, than were the once-divorced. Moreover, their physical and mental health was less good. As indicated in items 19 through 28 the multiply-divorced rated their current overall health as much less good, and had felt an impending nervous breakdown in the past year more frequently. They felt "down" more often, less in control of their lives, and were often tense. They also had taken more prescribed psychotropic drugs in the past two weeks, and had consumed more alcoholic beverages at one sitting. In addition, the multiply-divorced had been in treatment for emotional problems in the past year much more often, had been so treated after their first marriage more often and even so during their current marriage. In fact, in a separate study of the trajectory for treatment of emotional disorders in the overall sample, a multiplicity of divorces constituted the most salient main effect in a regression analysis (Ambert 1989). These statistics may explain why the multiply-divorced had had more often recourse to professionals for help (item 29). In addition, these statistics, as well as the ones about their family background, may indicate a causal relationship between their mental health and their recurrent marital dissolutions.

EX-SPOUSES OF THE ONCE-DIVORCED AND MULTIPLY-DIVORCED

Were the ex-spouses of the multiply-divorced similar or different from the ex-spouses of the once-divorced? In order to answer this question, I compared the two categories of ex-spouses on the same variables detailed in Table V.1. I was able to gather data on 36 of the 41 ex-spouses of the multiply-divorced, and on 159 ex-spouses of once-divorced persons.

In terms of sociodemographic characteristics, there were no statistically significant differences between the two categories of ex-spouses. There were, however, indications that the ex-spouses of the multiply-divorced tended to be still divorced rather than remarried. There also was a $p < .08$ difference indicating that ex-spouses of the multiply-divorced more frequently belonged to the categories of housekeepers and persons on welfare: slightly fewer were employed full-time (60% vs. 73%). This small difference stemmed from the fact that some of these ex-spouses were women who had been deserted and left with young children. Overall, the data suggest that any difference between these two sets of ex-spouses was the *consequence* of having been married to a multiply-divorced versus a once-divorced person. For instance, there was no age difference nor any large difference in terms of average schooling. There was no income difference between those who were gainfully employed. Finally, there was no difference in terms of familial background and happiness as teenagers.

There were no differences on the health variables. In the area of the past marriage, the ex-spouses of the multiply-divorced reported a lower marital happiness, but the difference was not statistically significant. And for those who were currently remarried, the only significant difference between the two groups emerged: ex-spouses of the multiply-divorced reported being *happier* in their current marriage than the other ex-spouses (4.8. vs. 4.3, t test: $p < .021$). Moreover, the standard deviation was much smaller for the ex-spouses of the multiply-divorced (.5 vs. .99).

Therefore, overall, little differentiated the two categories of ex-spouses in terms of *background*. The ex-spouses of the multiply-divorced did not appear to present a greater marital risk than the other spouses, unless themselves multiply-divorced. Persons of either category appeared to be randomly distributed and unrelated to the fact of having been married to a person divorced only once or divorced many times—except, perhaps, in terms of the socioeconomic consequences of such a circumstance, and feelings of satisfaction in a current remarriage.

DO THE EX-SPOUSES OF EACH PERSON RESEMBLE EACH OTHER?

Because there is some journalistic and anecdotal material indicating that divorce "recidivists" tend to "fall" for the same type of person over and over (Bohannan 1971), I had expected a great deal of similarity among the ex-spouses within each set. Therefore, I investigated whether the second ex-spouse resembled the first and whether the third one was a carbon copy of the other two. Because I was dealing with comparisons between two or three persons, statistical indicators were not suitable. Thus, the indicators used were physical appearance, deportment as I rated it after the interviews, overall personality as expressed through the interviews, and occupation. Data for 15 sets will be presented where at least two ex- spouses had been interviewed in a same set. This includes three males who had three ex-wives each; all the persons in these three sets were interviewed. In addition, 12 sets of two ex-spouses were interviewed.

In *all* cases, the ex-wives or the ex-husbands did not even remotely resemble each other physically, whether in hair color, complexion, or size. Physical appearance and self-presentation are the first cues which arouse another person's interest: obviously, most multiply-divorced had not chosen their spouses in terms of a fixed preference. For the ex-wives, another tangible indicator of their difference, rather than their similarity, was their age: within each set, subsequent ex-wives were currently younger than first ex-wives by at least 7 years. This age difference reinforced the difference in physical presentation: subsequent ex-wives were more youthful looking than the first at interview time. As will be shown, in Chapter VI, multiply-divorced men tended to have the largest age difference with their current spouse of all the respondents in the sample. Multiply-divorced women, however, tended more often to have ex-husbands close to each other in age.

In terms of deportment and overall personality as observed by this clinically trained researcher, there was only one case of similarity among ex-spouses: one woman had married serially two men who were congenial, thoughtful, and even charitable—one of whom was multiply-divorced. At Time 3, the woman was institutionalized for schizophrenia (she had already been in ambulatory treatment when interviewed at Time 2). Both ex-husbands, who were happily remarried, were cooperatively taking turns visiting her on a monthly basis to ensure that she was adequately cared for. At Time 3, the confused woman believed her two ex-husbands to be her brothers. But this intriguing story is just *one* outstanding and unrepresentative case. In the other cases, first and second (and even third) ex-spouses had little in common except for a former spouse they had shared serially. Moreover, *current* spouses were also very different from previous spouses and, if our indicators of marital stability are valid, a majority of these current spouses will one day become ex-spouses. It was actually uncanny how different a choice each multiply-divorced person had made each time he or she had remarried.

In conclusion, within each set of ex-spouses, differences were striking. These persons certainly shared traits, but they did so in the same manner that they would do with any other person interviewed in the sample. In other words, it was as if the ex-spouses had been randomly selected within each set. In fact, for most of them, it would have made more "sense" had they belonged to another set!

CAUSES OF DIVORCE
PERCEIVED BY THE EX-SPOUSES

The object of this section is to see whether a person's ex-spouses had had similar or different experiences with the spouse they had shared serially. In order to achieve this end, I used the question on the causes of marital breakup and compared the responses of the ex-spouses. Out of the 15 complete sets of ex-spouses, only 4 (or 27%) *disagreed* entirely on the causes of their own divorce to *their common ex-spouse.* The others agreed entirely, that is, gave *all* the same causes in two instances, and gave more than half the same causes in the rest of the cases.

The cases of overlap but no total agreement stemmed from the sequential nature of these relationships: for instance, more first ex-spouses mentioned financial problems than subsequent spouses because subsequent spouses tended to be more often employed, were younger, had no children from the multiply-divorced person, and thus were less dependent on that person's financial resources. More subsequent ex-spouses mentioned their own adultery as a cause of divorce than first ex-spouses did, perhaps because subsequent ex-spouses, especially wives, were younger, less patient, less dependent, understandably less trusting, and more willing to jeopardize a union which was already not satisfactory.

Each ex-spouse could give several reasons for the marital breakup. In all, 33 ex-spouses of 15 multiply-divorced persons answered this particular question. The following six main causes of marital dissolution stood out in their reports.

	number of times mentioned
ex-spouse's emotional problems	15
ex-spouse's drinking	11
ex-spouse's cruelty	10
financial problems	10
didn't get along	9
children	8

These causes, except for children and financial problems, were given *by at least two ex-spouses within each of the 15 complete sets.* Thus, the ex-spouse's emotional problems were mentioned in all 15 complete sets of ex-spouses and by at least two ex-spouses.

It is quite remarkable that, with the exception of "didn't get along" and "financial problems," the causes of marital dissolution given by these ex-spouses *were specific to that group*. In other words, although the 33 ex-spouses in the 15 complete sets represented only 16% of the entire sample of divorced persons, they provided over 40% of the mentions of emotional problems, drinking, cruelty, and children as main causes of their marital breakup. Thus, *not only did the ex-spouses of the multiply-divorced agree among themselves within each set on the causes of their divorces, but there are certain causes of marital breakdown which were over-reported by the ex-spouses of the multiply-divorced* (and under-reported by the ex-spouses of the once-divorced). In addition, these ex-spouses repeatedly used adjectives such as selfish, self-centered, and unstable to describe their multiply-divorced ex-spouse. There were also indications in the qualitative data that, *given sufficient time, the multiply-divorced made their spouses more miserable than the once-divorced* (or left their spouses more abruptly).

CAUSES OF DIVORCE PERCEIVED BY THE MULTIPLY-DIVORCED

The previously discussed material leads into a comparison of the perception of the multiply-divorced with that of their ex-spouses. So far, it has been shown that the ex-spouses were very congruent in describing the person they had shared serially, and the current new spouses generally concurred with the previous spouses (albeit, without knowing it). In this section, the answers provided by the multiply-divorced were compared with those of their first ex-spouses, their second ex-spouses and, then, third ex-spouses where applicable. This provided me with 36 usable sets of comparisons: 3 sets for comparisons with third ex-spouses; 17 sets for comparisons with second ex-spouses and 16 sets for comparisons with first ex-spouses. In 20/36 cases or 56% there was absolutely *no* agreement between the causes reported by the multiply-divorced persons and the causes reported by the one ex-spouse involved in the comparison. In 10/36 cases or 28% there was partial agreement and there was total agreement in only 4/36 cases or 11%. Thus, *overall, there was little agreement on causes of divorce between the multiply-divorced person and his/her ex-spouses*; in contrast, we saw that the ex-spouses (both within and across sets) tended to agree substantially in terms of their experience with these persons.

The following were six main causes of divorce recurring among the multiply-divorced respondents' reports:

	number of times mentioned
own boredom	12
sexual incompatibility	10
didn't get along	10
financial problems	10
grew apart	8
the children	7

Only three of these problems—("didn't get along," "financial problems," "the children")—were also considered to be major problems by the ex-spouses, although, except for children, the ex-spouses mentioned these proportionately less frequently. In contrast, boredom, sexual incompatibility, and grew apart were rarely mentioned by the ex-spouses, unless these ex-spouses had also been multiply-divorced (in which case they appear above as well). The problems stemming from children, however, were not of the same nature as those reported by the ex-spouses. While the ex-spouses were concerned about the effect multiply-divorced had on their children, the multiply-divorced had little patience for their stepchildren and even their children. (This fact is corroborated in an earlier section of this chapter where it was shown that the multiply-divorced were more distant from their children.) Generally, "own boredom" and "sexual incompatibility" meant that the other was in reality at fault; there were good reasons to be bored and to be incompatible sexually. It is also noteworthy that, although the multiply-divorced accounted for only 9.1% of the entire sample of divorced persons, they accounted for 26% of the mentions of own boredom. And the same proportion applies for sexual incompatibility.

A general complaint on the part of the ex-spouses and even current spouses consisted in a feeling of having been ensnared by great personal charm but of a temporary nature, never to be extended into the marriage itself. Many of the multiply-divorced subjects were reported to have the ability to become instantly the type of person sought by their dating partner. The latter could not resist the convincing "sales pitch," as one ex-spouse put it. Because the courtship period was brief, the role playing did not have to last very long. The end result was that the dating partner, having become a spouse, often woke up the next day with "another person," never again to experience the charming personality which he or she had loved.

In view of the fact that the multiply-divorced in this sample were very "marriage prone" and remarried much sooner after a divorce and after a shorter acquaintance than the once-divorced, it could well be that they acted more randomly in their selection process and consorted with whoever happened to be there at the time. They married this person instead of having a reasonable courtship period to test whether this person was suitable or not. It is as if getting married per se was more important to a majority of the multiply-divorced, while getting married to the *right* person may be more important to the once-divorced. Thus, in part, the cause for the fluctuating marital careers of multiply-divorced persons.

CASE STUDIES

This section will reveal how the results already described in his chapter present themselves in actual persons. The two case studies are taken from a same network as shown in the diagram on the following page.

The first case is that of Jennifer Cayhill, age 41, a head nurse who appears as number 1. Her first divorce was from Howard Morrison (number 2) in 1977 and she has custody of their two children age 18 and 15. In 1980, Jennifer remarried an already twice-divorced man, Garry Ford (number 6), and they separated the following year. Garry remarried that same year after a 3-month courtship to his current wife who is of Muslim background.

Jennifer Cayhill is a good example of a person who has become multiply-divorced "by association" rather than by propensity. By this, I mean that, during a period of crisis in her life, she hastily remarried a man who had already been twice divorced; she was his third wife. Garry, in contrast, is a person who is "divorce prone" (currently, he has a fourth wife), and he will be described later.

In 1984, Jennifer had been on her own for two years since her second divorce and was a well-adjusted divorcee, especially when

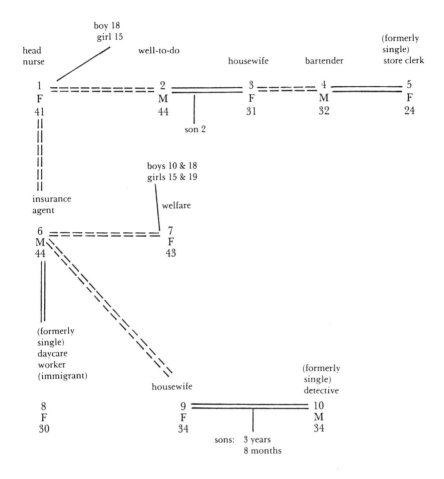

Notes: The broken lines indicate persons who are divorced from each other while the solid lines indicate current marriages. A straight line leads from the children to the parent they live with. Each respondent has been given a number in order to refer to the complicated structure of this network. The other number refers to each respondent's age.

compared to how she had been when I interviewed her in 1981. Even her children had improved greatly; her son was, in fact, completely different. The adolescents were poised, thoughtful, and pleasant. Of her children Jennifer said: "They are finally realizing how hard things have been for me and are much more appreciative. They try harder at school and help out more."

Her first divorce followed a "normal" course; they had grown apart and her husband "was too involved in his work." Their marriage had lasted 14 years. She says that her first ex-husband used to be closer to their children before he had a baby from his remarriage. Since then, her children have also done "some distancing of their own as they feel things are unfair." Although Howard is well-to-do, he pays even less for his children than he used to and the children resent their father's lavish lifestyle. Howard's remarriage has thus increased Jennifer's life difficulties financially (although she has a good income of her own) and for her children.

Jennifer is indifferent toward Howard and vacillates between indifference and dislike toward Garry. She never sees either of them, and speaks to Howard over the phone four times a year; the conversations are brief and strictly related to their children. In the following, Jennifer describes how she "descended" into her second marriage and divorce.

> All of a sudden, I realized I was growing older and things were not going too well with my daughter. My husband was remarrying, living the high life and had become less cooperative with the children. His wife is such a dumb blond stereotype. Anyway, I started dating more or less indiscriminately and met this really nice fellow who was so kind to me [Garry]. He was everything a woman could want ... One thing led to another and we were married after three months. At first, my children were happy because he was good to them but after he moved in he changed from one day to the next. I couldn't believe it. At first, he wasn't too bad to me but he no longer was his attentive self. But it was the children who really got on his nerves. He was bossing them around ... Then, he lost his job and was home for a month, not looking [for another job] too much. But we got lucky and he got another job because his first wife [number 7 in the diagram] kept pushing for child support. He had four kids from her.
>
> But his kids kept coming here because he didn't want to visit them at their place, of course, because he hated his ex-wife. We had six kids here at times ... the whole house was a mess for us to clean and the frig was empty and *I* had to pay. Then things got worse between him and me and I told him to change or else. I went to see a lawyer because I was afraid to lose the house but he said that, under the circumstances, no judge would rule against me. I was

slipping at work and one of the doctors suggested I see a psychiatrist and the kids started telling me I should throw him out.

It all sounds so simple now but I really agonized over it. You see, I was to be divorced for a second time and that's harder to take. It gives you a sense of personal failure. Anyway, I ended up packing up his things with the kids one day and we put everything in the garage and I had my lawyer draw up a separation agreement, and when he came back at night, I told him to leave. As it turned out, he moved in right away with a woman he had been carrying on with for the past couple of months. I was both relieved and mad at him. I was glad it was over so easily but I felt I had been really cheated. I haven't seen him since. I don't even know where he lives ... but his first ex-wife could tell you. Now, here's a woman I really feel sorry for ... I'd like to help her but I can't stand her children.

His second wife? Well, I didn't learn about her until we got married. He said it had been nothing, that she had left him, that she had been unfaithful. I believed him at the time but not now.

What's the future like for me? I'll probably stay single. I feel much better about this now... And I am financially secure... I mean, I don't have an exciting future ahead but it's quite decent. It's a lot better than what I can have with a bad husband. [She explained that her self-confidence had plummeted during her remarriage.] I was disgusted with myself for having allowed this marriage to happen to me.

Her second ex-husband, Garry Ford, age 44, is an insurance agent, and remarried in 1981 to Amina, a formerly-single daycare worker who emigrated to Canada on her own from England. She is Muslim, of Pakistani origin, and her family does not know she married a non-Muslim man.

As previously suggested, Garry has quite a long marital and divorce history. His first marriage lasted 16 years, his second 2, and the last to Jennifer, 1. He remained on his own for two years between marriages 1 and 2, only one year between marriages 2 and 3, and, after Jennifer, moved in right away with his current wife whom he admitted having dated while still married.

How does he feel about three divorces? "What about it? Nothing to be ashamed of, nothing to be proud of. Just bad luck, I suppose. I think I may be in luck this time. My wife and I are very compatible. She's no hassle. She isn't like the previous ones." His wife expressed many areas of dissatisfaction with their marriage, but felt that some were "outside of our control. We would have a child but he already has children. We could do more things but he's got to partly support his children [of which he does very little]. What should I ask for? The sky? My sisters married in their religion and their marriages aren't even as good as mine. In comparison to them, I am very lucky." She also feels that her husband is more stable than he used to be during his previous marriages. Above all, "I am not as independent as were his previous wives because I have been taught differently. I am a more suitable wife for him than the others were. I am patient and I don't ask for much. I have had a hard life and this life is good for me. If only I could have children of my own."

Garry's first wife (number 7 in the diagram) has custody of their four children age 10 to 19. Edwina is age 43, on welfare, but does occasional housework and sewing to supplement her income. She was pregnant when she married Garry at age 19, but the child was retarded and soon died. Garry gives very little toward the support of his children and certainly does not contribute to their upbringing. "When they do something wrong, he never says anything to them which forces me to nag the children." She has to phone him weekly and with meager results: "and then he accused me of being a nag" as she repeatedly has to beg for money. Edwina feels that his first two remarriages "were more of a problem because the children were younger and we were more desperate financially. Life was really hard then. I guess we're all used to him getting remarried."

"My children were really messed up. I don't know if it's my being divorced or all his remarriages. But you can't say that they have had a regular family life." She also points out that, when they were still together, "he was not a very good example. He used to drink and be quite loud and pushy and hard to get along with." Her oldest daughter is pregnant; Edwina is looking forward to being a grandmother but it also means that her daughter "will quit work and won't be able to help me anymore. But I might babysit for her for money if she can keep her job."

Garry used to threaten to leave. "He left many times and used to come back when he felt like it. Then he left again and didn't return." Although she has little to do with his current wife, she liked his previous one. Jennifer phones her once in a while:

We could have gotten along well but now that I think of it I am sure it was hard on her and her kids when mine used to go there. He used to invite them all the time and of course I loved it because it gave me some time by myself and she used to feed them real well but she resented it because he used to do it to spite her own kids because he hated them. I couldn't do anything about it so she didn't like me too much and I thought she was snotty but she called me back after she kicked him out and I thought it was real decent of her to do that so we got to talking and understanding each other better. But I don't think that wives can get along too well when there are problems like money and children. She doesn't phone me too often because she's probably afraid I would ask her to help me. I wouldn't but I can't blame her.

His other wife [number 9 on the diagram] didn't put up with the kids and she told me to keep them. I thought she was a real bitch. They were younger and I had so much trouble. She could have helped more but she was young and she didn't want to have to shoulder my problems. Besides, she didn't put up with him for long. *She* phoned me to tell me she had left and she said she didn't hate me but she just couldn't stand it. Then she called me back when her kids were born. I guess she wanted me to let him know to spite him. She really has a good husband and a new life. She's happy and I am happy for her but I wish I could be this lucky. But she had no kids and she was young so it was not difficult to start a better life at her age and she had a decent job.

Garry's second wife, about whom Edwina talks, is a 34-year-old former secretary, now a housewife remarried to a detective and the mother of two small boys age 3 and 8 months respectively. Sharon Corbett has been remarried for four years after a 10-month courtship period. She had been married to Garry for two years but had not been exactly faithful during that period. "I knew I wasn't going to stay with him for very long, and I started dating and I purposely avoided divorced men. One had been enough. I wanted a normal man without an ex-wife and without a herd of children. I wanted a real life and not the type that social workers like to talk about."

Sharon attributes the rapid downfall of her first marriage to Garry's drinking, emotional problems, his children, and her own infidelity. "As soon as I realized what the situation was going to be like, I got hold of myself, saw a lawyer friend, got myself a separate bank account and detached myself from the situation. I started planning ahead. You may think this crude and cold but it was what I *had* to do and I did it. I am the happier for it now. But my first marriage could have been very unhappy had I let it happen and if I had had children."

Why did shy marry Garry? "He was a very nice man. I gather he is always a nice man before he gets married but he changes as soon as he settles down. He didn't turn mean exactly, just indifferent. It's as if he was exhausted by all the effort he had put in while we were dating. You may not believe this but he is a very nice man when he wants to. He could charm a snake." She emphasizes that she probably would have never divorced had she married someone else: "I am not the divorcing type."

She also talked about Edwina. "Yes, I called his first wife when I had my children. I felt sorry for her but I didn't want to have anything to do with her while I was married to *our* ex-husband because I didn't want to have anything to do with all the children. I didn't like her then and she didn't like me either. What can you do? I had enough of my problems without hers. But after that she was no threat to me so I could talk to her once in a while."

These two case studies of two multiply-divorced persons well illustrate how complicated the life of the ex-spouse who has children becomes with each successive remarriage. The children move from one visiting stepmother to another during their young years. Although ex-wives 2 and 3 were in touch with ex-wife 1 occasionally as they both felt sorry for her, such a situation was not necessarily the rule in multiple divorces as indicated in an earlier section. Nevertheless, becoming a man's ex-wife frequently seemed to give rise to a certain bonding between ex-wives; this, however, occurred only *after* they had become ex-wives. The feeling of empathy did not generally arise while one of them was still the legal wife. Ex-husbands of a multiply-divorced woman did not develop such ex-spousal networks, perhaps because these women did not have children as a general rule, perhaps because men do not partake as easily as women of such quasi-kin relationships.

It may also be noticed how difficult it is to keep track of who is who vis-a-vis whom in these case studies. One easily forgets the sequential order of the ex-spouses and one easily becomes confused in the various entanglements of dyads, triads, ex-dyads, and so on.

Often, while I was doing the interviews, I had the strange feeling of watching a soap program. I had great difficulty memorizing who was what and often had an existential feeling of the absurd, dealing with numbers rather than persons. These researcher's reactions stemmed in part from the confusing nature of the situation and of the various interactions; but it probably stemmed also from the level of deviance from the norm which these scenarios presented compared to the less complicated situations of once-divorced persons. Finally, as I progressed from one multiply-divorced person, especially man, to another, there was a growing feeling of déjà vu. The men's stories were somewhat repetitive and much more uniform than those coming from the once-divorced. Their ex-spouses' reactions were also more similar than those of other ex-spouses so that all these scenarios blended into a relatively repetitive *novella*.

CONCLUSIONS

In summary, the multiply-divorced were substantially different from the once-divorced in terms of familial background, personal qualities, and personal relations. They were more unstable persons, and had more personality problems, a perception shared by their ex-spouses. However, their ex-spouses were not different from the ex-spouses of the once-divorced, indicating that marital instability could not generally be causally related to these ex-spouses. In addition, *within each set* of ex-spouses, there was little personality similarity, again refuting any hypothesis that the ex-spouses were high risk persons and, also, refuting the notion that the multiply-divorced sought the same type of person over and over. Rather, the data indicate that the multiply-divorced were marriage prone and remarried quickly to just about anyone at random. They were repeating previous "mistakes," not necessarily in their *choice* of partners, but in their attitude toward marriage and divorce. *Once remarried, they were generally less involved in their relationship and saw it as less stable than did the once-divorced who were remarried at the time of the interview* (see Byrd and Smith 1988; Counts and Reid 1987).

Moreover, within sets of ex-spouses, there was substantial agreement, in spite of their personality differences, concerning the spouse they had shared serially and the causes of the divorce. The causes agreed upon generally focused on dysfunctional personality traits and behaviors on the part of the multiply-divorced person. This suggests that the multiply-divorced were repeating their behavior and dragging the same unchanged personality and attitudes from one marriage to the next.

The multiply-divorced, with four exceptions, showed indicators of emotional instability, self-centeredness, inability to form deep attachment, inability to adapt at the inter-personal level, and lack of empathy (and even of sympathy). Such personality traits can more logically be causally related to multiple-divorce than vice versa (Brody et al. 1988). For instance, three respondents who redivorced between Times 2 and 3 had exhibited such traits *before* their redivorce. Therefore, *it will be hypothesized that individuals, with the personality or attitudinal problems as herein described, who also have the ability to attract men/women to them present a particularly high risk of repeated marital disruption.* Blood and Blood (1978) have already concluded that emotional problems constitute a risk factor toward multiple divorce. The ability to attract partners is, naturally, a *sine qua non*, for, indeed, the sample included a few other persons who resembled these multiply-divorced persons but who were alone and were unable to attract or retain a partner long enough to remarry.

However, it is imperative to emphasize that this hypothesis might be of no value in social circles that foster and/or are indulgent toward multiple divorces. Indeed, except in certain social circles and occupations, multiple divorces are not as acceptable as single divorces; they constitute deviant behavior in our society.[1] Because none of the subjects belonged to a social circle that fostered or even tolerated multiple divorces, it is reasonable to assume that a selection process entered here.

It is further hypothesized that persons who divorce serially *within a short time span* show consistency of behavior from marriage to marriage while persons who divorce and remarry only once within the same period of time exhibit a certain degree of functional change where necessary, or else finally find a spouse who will conform to their idiosyncrasies (or find a person who is a lower risk). Therefore, persons with multiple divorces *within a short time span* probably fail both to change (Cherlin 1978) and to find spouses who would accept or fit their idiosyncrasies.

The number of multiply-divorced in this sample was small, but the differences with the once-divorced were extremely large and generally congruent with the results reported in Fox's (1983) study (except demographically), although the conclusions reached are not necessarily identical. Other results were corroborated in Counts and Reid (1987). Therefore, overemphasizing the defect in the sample size may be counter productive, not only because of the two reasons just mentioned, but also because the technical difficulties inherent to such a study should not be underestimated. Locating ex-spouses of separated/divorced subjects is already difficult (Newcombe 1984); but locating all the ex-spouses in a particular case of multiple-divorce is time consuming and costly. Also, the multiply-divorced, especially the men, were more uncooperative than once-divorced persons. The research design involving interviews with their ex-spouses clearly irritated and threatened them while the once-divorced were generally very cooperative and even interested in all phases of the study. Such methodological complications are unfortunate because multiple divorces are rising along with the general increase in divorce and, as this report only begins to suggest, we suffer from almost total ignorance on this topic.

From a clinical perspective, the ex-spouses of the multiply-divorced, especially the first ex-spouses, had generally been more traumatized than ex-spouses of the once-divorced. The children of the multiply-divorced also had more problems (as observed and coded at Time 1) and these problems seemed to last longer than those of children of single divorces. Few saw their multiply-divorced parent. Moreover, such children had the added burden of identifying or rejecting one parent whose behavior is confusing and socially unacceptable.

It could be advanced that courts should request persons undergoing a second or third divorce within a short time span to seek counselling. Such a situation may appear to go against an individual's rights but the rights of children and of subsequent spouses who may suffer from this marital dislocation should also be considered. Especially useful might be clinical interventions which would help the multiply-divorced take "time out" of the marriage market to reconsider their goals, lives, and options, and to educate them so as to increase their marital skills and their level of ability to commit themselves to a marital partner. Indeed, it could be advanced that divorce is a learned behavior that has obviously become easier for these persons to put into practice than adaptive marital behavior.

NOTE

1. There is so little research on the topic of multiple divorces that I could not find any public opinion survey on attitudes toward multiple divorces in this Metropolitan area.

Chapter VI

Age Difference in Remarriage

I like my husband being older [8 years older]. If he were my age then I would be too old for him. This way, I feel secure.

—Woman, housewife, age 43

When a man gets remarried, if he can't afford a younger wife, he is not a man.

—Man, skilled worker, age 37

I may not want children now but what if I do in ten years? He'll be nearly 60 and ready to retire. His age will close doors for me, there is no question about that.

—Woman, career, age 28

I used to think that a woman my age was too old for me. I dated much younger women, you know the stereotypical bachelor. I liked the ego boost these girls gave me. But when the party was over and time came to face life, I went for a woman my age ... otherwise the life goals, long-term life goals, would have been too different.

—Man, professional, age 44

This chapter focuses on age difference in remarriages following divorce. Large age gaps between husbands and wives in remarriages or in marriages in which one spouse is remarrying after divorce have already been noted (Dean and Gurak 1978; Rossi 1980; Spanier 1983, p. 284; Vera et al. 1985). However, the ramifications of remarriage among persons who actually belong to different age cohorts have yet to be explored. In societies in which women are traditionally subordinate to and dependent on men, an age gap in which the husband is much older may be functional for the marital unit, the husband, and perhaps even the woman. However, in a society which theoretically and legally supports gender equality, in which a majority of the married women are gainfully employed, and in which a companionate marriage is the ideal, it could logically be expected that a large age gap between spouses might lead to difficulties for one of them and even for the marriage itself (Atkinson and Glass 1985).

Aguirre and Parr (1982) found that, for women in a first marriage, the most important predictor of marital instability was a husband's previous divorce, while no such a predictor existed for men. I wondered if Aguirre and Parr's findings might not be in part related to age differentials. But I could not find any systematic treatment of this topic in the literature, although one study shows that *marriages* are less stable when there is a large age difference (Glick 1980). Moreover, studies indicate that, in general, remarriages are less homogamous than first marriages (Dean and Gurak 1978; Rosenthal 1970) and are also less stable (Cherlin 1977; Hoffman and Holmes 1976; McCarthy and Menken 1978; Norton and Glick 1976; Plateris 1979). In a study of separations, Kitson (1985) found that couples who were less than five years apart were more likely to reconcile than others with a larger age difference. It would therefore be important to know the role of age homogamy in the stability and even success of remarriages since age homogamy has been related to *stability* of first marriages (Bumpass and Sweet 1972; Nye and Berardo 1973). These conclusions, however, are not unanimously shared as data presented by Jorgensen and Klein (1979) and Vera et al. (1985) did not exhibit any relationship between age heterogamy and marital quality (see, also, Rogler and Procidano 1989).

In addition, it has been established that *marriages* with a large age difference are more likely to occur among lower-SES persons (Atkinson and Glass 1985; Vera et al. 1985). Moreover, the older a man is at marriage, the larger the age gap with his new wife (Glick and Norton 1977; Spanier and Glick 1980).

This chapter will first use the data to see if the demographic results of these few previous studies will apply. Then, at a more analytical level, how remarried couples perceive their age differencee or heterogamy will be examined. Do they perceive it as problematic for the future and, if so, what types of problems do they foresee? In age-heterogamous remarriages, do both spouses foresee problems or do men and women differ in their perceptions? Then, how does age similarity/difference relate to current marital happiness and to anticipated long-term marital stability? And, finally, at the *couple level*, how does similarity of perception (or congruence) on anticipated problems relate to current marital happiness and perceived long-term marital stability at the individual level (see Laumann 1966; Verbrugge 1966)?

GENERAL AGE DIFFERENCES

The focus in on 197 persons, who are part of 103 remarriages. These 197 persons include the 163 remarried subjects in this sample as well as 34 other subjects who were in a first marriage as new spouses of some of these remarried respondents. Table VI.1., shows that 66% of the 103 remarriages in the study consisted of two persons who had been previously married (10% of whom included one formerly-widowed person remarried to a previously-divorced subject). The rest of the remarriages included one never-married person: nearly twice as many previously single women as single men were included in this category. This latter difference reflects divorced men's slightly greater propensity to marry a single woman than divorced women to marry a single man (Schlesinger 1979). But above all, this trend is an artifact of the age structure of the sample: had more divorced women in the 20- to 30-age-bracket been included, a higher proportion of women remarried to single men would have been obtained (Statistics Canada 1981).

The average age difference was 6.7 years. In remarriages that included a divorced man and a single woman, the average age difference was 9.3 years when the man was older. However, when a divorced woman had remarried a single man who was younger, he was so by an average of only 4.6 years or half the age difference in a divorced man/single woman combination. When both spouses had been previously married, the average age difference involved an older husband in 78% of the cases with an average age gap of 8 years, and in 22% of the cases, a slightly older woman or a woman of the same age. Moreover, the 13 persons who were in a third or fourth marriage were older than their new spouse by an average of 11.2 years.

Table VI.1. Age Difference (Averages and Frequencies)
in Remarriages Including One and Two Remarried Spouses

| | | | Remarriages Including One Previously Single Person | | | |
| | Remarriages Including Two Remarried Spouses* | | Man Remarried to Single Woman | | Woman Remarried to Single Man | |
	N	$\bar{X}$ Age Difference Years	N	$\bar{X}$ Age Difference Years	N	$\bar{X}$ Age Difference Years
Men older	53	8.0	23	9.3	2	1.0
Women older	9	3.0	0	—	7	4.6
Same age	6	N.A.	0	N.A.	3	N.A.
Totals	68		23		12	
Percentage of remarriages						
($N = 103$)	66%		22.3%		11.7%	

Notes: * Including 10 previously-widowed spouses of previously-divorced respondents.

This brief summary points to a large age gap in the remarriages in this sample, as has been the case in other studies, especially in multiple remarriages, and in remarriages involving a divorced man with a single woman. When two previously-married spouses were involved, the gap was still substantial but somewhat smaller. The combination that seemed to allow for the greatest chance of either age homogamy or of a reversed age difference was that of a divorced woman with a single man, perhaps because it was generally younger divorcees who had contracted such unions.

AGE DIFFERENCES:
AGE AT REMARRIAGE AND SES

In Table VI.2, where age at remarriage is used as a basis of analysis, we see that the remarriage percentages for women fell drastically after age 35. In fact, remarried women were five years younger than unremarried women (36 vs. 41) while there was no difference among remarried and unremarried men. That age is a crucial determinant of a divorced woman's remarriageability has been documented (Carter and Glick 1976; Cornell 1989; Gurak and Dean 1979; Spanier and Glick 1980). Above all, Table VI.2

Table VI. 2. Average Age Differences by Age at Remarriage and Direction of Differences

	Men's Age at Remarriage (N = 88)										Women's Age at Remarriage (N = 80)									
	-30		30-35		36-40		41-45		46+		-30		30-35		36-40		41-45		46+	
	(N)	$\bar{X}$ Diff.	(N)	$\bar{X}$ Diff.	(N)	$\bar{X}$ Diff.	(N)	$\bar{X}$ Diff.	(N)	$\bar{X}$ Diff.	(N)	$\bar{X}$ Diff.	(N)	$\bar{X}$ Diff.	(N)	$\bar{X}$ Diff.	(N)	$\bar{X}$ Diff.	(N)	$\bar{X}$ Diff.
Men older	(9)	5.2	(17)	5.4	(19)	8.3	(21)	9.6	(7)	15.6	(23)	8.0	(20)	7.6	(7)	5.1	(2)	19.0	(2)	8.0
Women older	(3)	2.0	(1)	4.0	(3)	2.7	(0)	NA	(2)	4.5	(2)	1.0	(6)	4.7	(6)	3.3	(1)	4.0	(2)	4.5
Same age	(0)	NA	(2)	NA	(4)	NA	(0)	NA	(0)	NA	(3)	NA	(2)	NA	(4)	NA	(0)	NA	(0)	NA
Totals	(12)		(20)		(26)		(21)		(9)		(28)		(28)		(17)		(3)		(4)	
Intra-sex (%)	13.6%		23%		29.5%		24%		10%		35%		35%		21%		3.8%		5%	

111

indicates that a woman's age at remarriage bore little relationship with her spousal age gap while the contrary occurred for men: men older at remarriage had a larger age difference with their wives than had younger men. This is well in accordance with results obtained by Glick and Norton (1977) and Spanier and Glick (1980).

I also wanted to see if there would be class variations in age differences at remarriage, as other studies have found larger age differences in first marriages at the lower-SES level.[1] I examined the class variable using *both* men's and women's SES as the baselines. *Current* SES was used as I had no accurate data on SES at remarriage. However, I do not believe that this procedure represents a bias because respondents had been remarried for an average of over 2 years only—not sufficient time to allow for a great deal of social mobility.

Table VI.3 replicates the results of other studies in that lower-SES men had younger wives than middle-SES and even higher-SES men. Moreover, 20.5% of the higher-SES men had married a woman their age or slightly older while only 8% of lower-SES men had done so. Therefore, higher-SES and middle-SES men were more age homogamous in their remarriages than lower-SES men, even when age was controlled for. However, using women's SES as a baseline, I found a reverse relationship: higher-SES women had more often married a same-age man or a man slightly younger rather than an older man. Indeed of the 16 higher-SES women who had remarried, 9 or 56% were remarried to a same-age man or were even older than their partner. If one higher-SES woman married to a man 21 years her senior (but also of higher-SES) is eliminated, the age difference falls to a drastic 3.5 from the higher 7. Thus, higher-SES women were less likely to be remarried to a much older man than women from the other classes and, especially, than previously-single women married to a divorced man.

Thus, while higher-SES women were less in a hurry to remarry (Ambert 1982), and remarried less during a given time period, holding age constant (Carter and Glick 1976), those who did remarry were the respondents who were the most age homogamous in their remarriages. They were also very class homogamous, thus contributing to explain why higher-SES men were also class homogamous when they married wives *close to them in age*. But higher-SES men who married out of their SES tended to have a large age difference over their younger wives (who were likely to

Table VI.3. Average Age Differences by SES and Direction of Differences

| | Men's SES | | | | | | Women's SES | | | | | |
| | Higher* | | Middle | | Lower | | Higher | | Middle | | Lower | |
	(N)	$\bar{X}$ Diff.	(N)	$\bar{X}$ Diff.	(N)	$\bar{X}$ Diff.	(N)	$\bar{X}$ Diff.	(N)	$\bar{X}$ Diff.	(N)	$\bar{X}$ Diff.
Men older	(35)	8.7	(27)	7.2	(11)	9.9	(7)	7.0	(29)	7.6	(18)	8.0
Women older	(5)	2.6	(3)	4.3	(1)	1.0	(5)	2.4	(8)	4.3	(4)	2.3
Same age	(4)	NA	(2)	NA	(0)	NA	(4)	NA	(5)	NA	(0)	NA
Totals	(44)		(32)		(12)		(16)		(42)		(22)	
Intra-sex (%)	50%		36%		14%		20%		53%		28%	

Note: * Higher corresponds to upper-middle class and lower-upper class. There were no upper-upper class respondents.

have been previously single) and in some cases provided the latter with an opportunity for a substantial upward social mobility— of 2 to 4 points on the 7-point scale (Mueller and Pope 1980).

AGE DIFFERENCES AND TYPES OF PROBLEMS

Each remarried and married respondent was asked if he/she was older, younger than, or the same age as the current spouse. Then, given an age difference of 5-7 years, I asked: "Do you think this age difference will create problems eventually in your marriage? Yes .. . no ..." And the same question was asked of those with a gap of more than seven years. If their answer was positive, they were requested to provide as many reasons as they deemed necessary from a pre-tested list.

- I will feel insecure because I will be so much older.
- My spouse will feel insecure because he/she will be so much older.
- We will have different ideas based on age.
- One of us may not be so healthy as the other.
- I may want to do things that my spouse would not want.
- My spouse may want to do things that I would not want.
- We may have different age-related problems.
- We may have different work-related problems.
- We may have different sexual capabilities.
- My spouse may be unfaithful to me.
- I may be unfaithful to my spouse.

Of the 28 *persons* who had 5-7 years difference with their current spouse, only 5 or 18% felt that this difference would eventually create problems in their marriage. However, of the 89 persons who had more than 7 years difference, 46 or 52% believed that the age difference would create problems. Consequently, the larger the age gap, the more likely respondents were to perceive potential problems. I then wanted to see which gender would perceive the situation as more or less problematic. First, we see in Table VI.4 that, with a difference of 5-7 years, men tended to see problems more often than women. (These men were generally married to women older than they.) But this gender difference is not

Table VI.4. Frequency of Men and Women
Who Perceived Problems by Age Difference

	5 to 7 Years Difference[a]				8+ Year Difference[b]			
	Men		Women		Men		Women	
	N	%	N	%	N	%	N	%
Perceived problems	4	31	1	7	18	40	28	64
Did not perceive problems	9	69	14	93	27	60	16	36
Totals	13		15		45		44	

Notes: [b] $p < .097$.
         [b] $p < .026$.

statistically significant and these men mentioned only an average of 2.7 problems. For the 89 respondents with a large age gap, there was a complete reversal of this trend; two-thirds of the women foresaw problems while one-third of the men did. (Such wide age gaps involved a younger woman married to a man who was much older than she; only two cases involved an older woman.)

At the 8 years and plus age gap, women mentioned more problems than men: 5.3 versus 4.6. Moreover, married women mentioned more problems than remarried women (5.7 vs. 3.9 problems). The one problem most frequently mentioned by both men and women focused on potential health problems. Then, women mentioned the possibility that each spouse may want to do different things while men mentioned that they may have different sexual capabilities. The third problem for women resided in the area of different sexual capabilities; men emphasized wanting to do different things. For women, the fourth problem mentioned was having different ideas based on age-related experience; for men it was having different age problems. It is also interesting that more women mentioned that they might be unfaithful (their fifth mention); only three men made such a mention while men stressed their wives' future unfaithfulness.

The following is a sample of respondents' explanations concerning their feelings toward their large age difference and the problems such a difference created or would create for them. For younger wives, the age difference translated into different expectations related to their respective age cohorts.

> It's not the age difference which worries me but the mentality difference. My husband is perfectly happy as things stand. He likes a boring life. He sits there perfectly contented with the tube and the newspapers. He is in the travel business but he doesn't even like to travel. I foresee problems when he retires because I will be active and he will be around the house alone and then I'll have to cater to him and start another period of motherhood and I feel that I have had more than enough children. (43-year-old woman remarried to 48-year-old man)

The next excerpt is from a 32-year-old remarried woman about her first husband who was twenty years her senior.

> He was too old for me and he had these girls [his daughters], real rude and uneducated. Spoiled and we didn't get along. Then he decided he didn't want to make so much money at *his* age, so I said: "what about my age? You may be near death but I am not. I need to be financially secure." ... I just got so disgusted, an old man, my father's age, playing at being young and not being able to. I had too much energy for him.

The next two comments are from men older than their wives, and these comments are very different in nature from those of the women previously quoted. It is also very noteworthy that, generally, men with younger wives provided very little conversational material on this topic while their younger wives dwelled on it. Older men generally accepted their age difference as a given; they rarely questioned it.

> It is good for a man to have a younger wife because he can have children into his old age and because she can take care of him. It's an advantage, not a problem. (38-year-old man remarried to a 26-year-old woman)

> The only unforeseen event is whether or not we will have children. We've discussed that as well. She'd have to raise the child on her own because I feel that I have lived too long without being a parent to start now and my work wouldn't allow it. (50-year-old man remarried to a 29-year-old woman)

What about situations in which the wife is actually older? One such a woman reported that her husband had wanted to get married before they actually did but she had kept postponing it because *she* was very concerned about their age difference (8 years) and what her family would think. "My family didn't like it at first but they have gotten used to it. Actually they think we're only four years apart. I never told them the exact truth. He looks older so no one has any reason to question it." Her son and ex-husband also thought that the new husband was only four years younger.

One 52-year-old man married to a woman two years his senior explained that it was important to him to marry a woman close to him in age because he wanted "stability, someone who understood my family problems, and I was tired of playing the young scene. I wanted to grow up, have a real life. I was tired of the rat race. I wanted someone who was not bitter, was not a gold digger, someone I could retire with." But, in his pursuit of equality, he had to surmount deeply-ingrained cultural stereotypes:

> Meeting my wife helped me a lot although I didn't ask her out right away; I had an inner struggle. I knew I wanted a woman closer to me in age but I was still too brainwashed by the idea of younger women so that at first I rejected the idea of going out with her. But I kept running into her at these friends' place and she was so comfortable to be with, so relaxed, not socially conscious, that I finally found her attractive and the more I took her out, the more attractive she became. I was very juvenile when I think of it. I was actually afraid of being with a woman my age and even of being *seen* with a woman my age. *This was tantamount to a social demotion* ... Oh yes, my first wife had one of her tactful reactions. She *smiled* but ... my ex-wife could never understand why I chose an older [two years older] woman even though she herself complains that men my age prefer younger women. She's too caught up in appearances, social acceptability, and whatever.

For many respondents, age differences presented no threat, although few women actually saw advantages to the situation. Many persons expressed the opinion that it was not the age difference per se which was problematic but the level of the spouses' maturity. Altruism was a quality frequently mentioned as a necessary ingredient for a successful marriage when a wide gap existed: "We complement each other and neither of us is so self-centered as to be unable to adjust to an age difference." Several women stressed what sociologists label anticipatory socialization as preventative against future problems. At that point, one notes the heightened level of consciousness concerning post-retirement years.

> My husband is older so that I am aware that I may be left alone again one day and this time I am actively preparing for this. (53-year-old woman remarried to a 66-year-old man)

> Well, I may be tempted to complain in fifteen years but I will not because I will be able to remember the good times that my husband has given me and how kind he has been to my children. I'll take good care of him when he is older. In fact I am going back to school this September. First, I'll finish high school and then might get some training at something so that I can support us when he's older and out of work. (34-year-old woman remarried to a 50-year-old man)

AGE DIFFERENCE, MARITAL HAPPINESS, AND STABILITY

For each respondent, I related the age gap to his/her marital happiness and anticipated likelihood that he/she would still be married to the same person in ten years from now. Table VI.5 shows that, as the age difference increases, men and women report a lower marital happiness (a lower score reflects a higher marital happiness). The level of increase was similar for both genders, and as in other studies women were somewhat less happy than men in all categories (e.g., White 1979). Although the differences may appear small, they were actually large when we pass from the first age category to the third because, overall, the respondents tended to rate their marital happiness highly, as a result perhaps of having been married only for an average of two years.

In terms of anticipated marital stability, the decline was noticeable only at the 8+ years gap and was substantial for women only. Therefore, women who were in marriages with men much older than they, not only tended to anticipate more problems than men (Table VI.4), especially if this was their first marriage, but

Table VI.5. Marital Happiness and Perceived
Matital Stability by Age Difference or Homogamy

	0 to 4 Year Difference		3 to 5 Year Difference		8+ Year Difference		
	$\bar{X}$	N	$\bar{X}$	N	$\bar{X}$	N	Sign
Marital happiness[a]							
men	1.4	36	1.7	22	1.8[c]	36	p < .02
women	1.6	40	1.8	19	2.1	38	p < .01
Marital stability[b]							
men	7.6	36	7.6	22	7.2[d]	35	n.s.
women	7.5	39	7.4	19	6.7	38	p < .05

Notes: [a] 1 = very high; 5 = very low.
[b] 1 = lowest; 8 = highest.
[c] Difference between men and women: p < .05.
[d] Difference between men and women: p < .01.
All other gender comparisons were nonsignificant.

felt less happy than other women in their marriage and less secure in terms of its potential stability (Table VI.5).

To pursue the comparison of remarried versus married women, I found no difference in terms of marital happiness for those who had a 8+ years spread with their spouses, but married women (N = 13) were significantly more skeptical concerning the longevity of their marriage than remarried women (N = 24): 6.1 and 7.2 respectively (p < .01).2. This difference stemmed in part both from the generally younger age of the women who were in their first marriage and their wider age gap with their older husbands. Although the N was small when further subdivided, there were indications that a younger age seemed to make a woman less tolerant, whether she was married or remarried. Therefore, because women in first marriages were younger by 8 years than those in remarriages, this age difference could explain in part why married women were less tolerant than remarried women.

Vera et al. (1985) have recently suggested that any correlation between age difference and marital unhappiness could actually be an artifact of class because persons of lower SES tend to be both age heterogamous and maritally unhappy more frequently than persons of higher SES. I tested for this possibility. As predicted, lower-SES persons, especially women, reported being maritally unhappy significantly more than higher-SES persons (as seen in Chapter VI). But this SES difference held both in cases of age similarity and difference, and, furthermore, actually decreased with a large age gap (8+ years). Thus, among persons who were more than seven years apart from their spouses in Table VI.5, there were no statistically significant differences in marital happiness and stability between those of lower and of higher SES. Consequently, the relationship between marital unhappiness and a large age gap is not an artifact of class in this sample.

PERCEPTION OF PROBLEMS:
DYADIC AND INDIVIDUAL PERSPECTIVES

This section focuses on the dyads and the individuals within the dyads for couples with an age gap of 8+ years. First, Table VI.6 indicates that there was more agreement than disagreement among the spouses as to whether or not they anticipated problems later on in life because of their large age gap: 28 couples agreed (congruent) and 14 disagreed (noncongruent). In 13 of the 28 congruent couples, neither spouse anticipated any problem whereas both spouses anticipated problems in the other 15 congruent couples. Among the 14 noncongruent couples there were only 3 in which husbands but not wives foresaw problems, but 11 in which wives foresaw problems while husbands did not. Looking at these data from another angle, only 13 couples did not anticipate problems at all while one or both spouses anticipated problems in the 29 other couples (32% vs. 69% of the couples).

How happy were the *individuals* with their marriage and how stable did they see it depending on what type of couple they belonged to? For marital happiness, both men and women belonging to couples in which both spouses foresaw age-related problems reported a much lower marital happiness. This was especially obvious among the men. But women who belonged to couples in which only the wives perceived problems had the lowest level of marital happiness of all individuals. The highest level of marital happiness was found among couples in which neither spouse anticipated problems or when husbands only anticipated problems.

121

Table VI.6. Marital Happiness and Perceived Marital Stability by Inter-spousal Congruence on Problems Related to Large Age Differences[a]

| | Congruent Couples (N = 28) | | | | | | Noncongruent Couples (N = 14) | | | | | | ANOVAS |
| | Both Spouses Do Not See Any Problem | | | Both Spouses See Problems | | | Only Men See Problems | | | Only Women See Problems | | | |
	$\bar{X}$	s.d.	N	$\bar{X}$	s.d.	N	$\bar{X}$	s.d.	N	$\bar{X}$	s.d.	N	sign
Marital happiness[b]													
men	1.2	.6	13	2.4	.9	15	1.3	.6	3	1.5[d]	.7	11	$p < .001$
women	1.4	.9	13	2.1	1.0	15	1.3	.6	3	2.5[d]	.9	11	$p < .001$
Marital stability[c]													
men	7.7	.8	13	6.7	1.4	15	8.0	0	3	7.4[d]	1.1	10	$p < .01$
women	7.5	1.9	13	6.4	1.8	15	8.0	0	3	6.5[d]	1.8	11	$p < .001$

Notes: [a] Includes only those couples with a difference of over seven years.
[b] 1 = very high; 5 = very low.
[c] 1 = lowest; 8 = highest.
[d] Comparison between men and women: $p < .001$. All other gender differences were nonsignificant using t tests.

The variable of marital stability, not unexpectedly, followed essentially the same pattern: those who were the least certain that they would still be with their current spouse in ten years belonged to couples in which both spouses foresaw age-related problems or in couples in which only the wives did so. In the latter case, it was mainly the wives who were pessimistic about their future together. In comparison, men were more optimistic.

DISCUSSION

The results in this chapter clearly indicate the importance of examining age differences in couples who are divorcing after a remarriage. Such an approach could help determine whether the greater feeling of marital instability reported by younger women married to much older men eventually translates into divorce or redivorce. Because of the paucity of the literature, it is impossible at this point to benefit from past research in order to speculate on other short-term and even long-term effects of large age differences between spouses in remarriages. One such an effect could be presumed on childbearing in remarriage: Griffith et al. (1985) report that a woman remarrying a man older than she considerably reduces her likelihood of having another child.

Many of the spouses in this research were keenly aware of belonging to different age cohorts and some of them already were experiencing related difficulties. As illustrated in the conversational material, they felt that they were at a stage of life different from that of their spouse and, because of this *décalage*, tensions were rising as not all age-related expectations could be met simultaneously. For instance, a man who had already raised a family and believed that once has been more than enough could not fulfill his younger wife's wish for a child unless he did so at the expense of *his* happiness. Or a woman who was building a career after years at home did not want to interrupt it just because her new husband was about to harvest the fruits of his own longer career and retire. Therefore, large age gaps were bringing irreconcilable goals and conflicting life requisites.

It has been shown that the partner who was the most likely to be affected by a large age gap was the younger woman who became doubly unequal in the relationship: female and younger, thus less experienced and generally less well established in the world. Also, because of recent social changes, younger women may have more individual goals and expectations than older women. These results concerning younger women are interesting from yet another perspective: Glenn and Weaver (1977) and White (1979) have found that married women reported a higher level of marital happiness than remarried women. However, in this sample, we see that married women expressed more skepticism about their marital stability than remarried women when married to a man older than they. Therefore, the matters of age and age homogamy may be crucial (see, also, Bytheway 1981; Peters 1979).

Women in a first marriage to a previously-divorced man probably are in a less enviable position than those who are married to a man who is also in a first marriage. This possibility seems very obvious yet the ramifications for marital life have not been explored. The issue of single persons marrying a divorced person is generally briefly discussed in the small but growing literature on stepparenting discussed in Chapter VII. But this differential stepparenting experience is merely one of the many research directions which can be taken in this respect. It would be important to study the entire range of differences in marital life which may exist for a single person marrying another single person compared to one marrying a divorced or widowed individual.

Among several of this sample's couples, the younger and attractive woman experienced upward social mobility upon marriage to a much older man. Therefore, in terms of exchange theory, a wide age gap presents both spouses with advantages depending on the resources which are the most important and bring the most returns for one or both partners (Blau 1964). However, this situation was more likely to achieve such an equilibrium of returns in decades of greater gender inequality where the male role as *the* head of the family was unquestioned and a young wife could reap rewards in having an older husband and starting a new family for him. Trends toward greater gender equality make this equilibrium more problematic as an older husband may not be sufficient enough a resource for a younger woman who could find another husband were she to divorce and who, at any rate, may be successful on the labor market on her own (Atkinson and Glass 1985). The older husband becomes a liability rather than an asset when he is perceived by the wife as not offering her the relationship and the lifestyle she wants. It is interesting in this respect that, along with trends toward gender equality, there has been in North America a trend toward greater age homogamy over the decades (Atkinson and Glass 1985; Kalbach and McVey 1976, p. 95); moreover, cross-cultural studies indicate that, in polygynous societies where women's subjugation is higher, husbands are much older than their wives.

Finally, there were faint indications in the current study that men remarried to a woman five years older might also be less happy maritally, although, contrary to women with an older man, they did not perceive their marriage to be less stable than the other men did. Overall, the data indicate that a relatively large age heterogamy in either direction is related to a lower marital happiness and a greater perceived marital instability—and that this is not a product of class differences. Therefore, it would be very important to do an in-depth comparison of the marital and divorce careers of couples who are age homogamous and age heterogamous, and, in the latter case, with women who are younger and women who are older. Because age-heterogamous wives (and some husbands as well) were less happy in their marriage and less confident of its stability, age heterogamy is herein seen as a liability, especially to women who are younger. The dynamics of this liability and its consequences deserve further attention.

NOTES

1. Social class, or SES, criteria are detailed in the notes of Chapter II.
2. Respondents were asked how likely it was that they would still be married to their current spouse 10 years hence. Completely likely = 8 to a zero possibility = 1.

Chapter VII

The New Spouses and Their Stepparenting Experience

I never dreamt I would ever be a stepmother. Who thinks about this when growing up?

—Stepmother, housewife

I love my stepchildren. Now I have a very large family and more grandchildren.

—Housewife, with married stepchildren

No, we don't have any [children]. Besides, his daughters come here every so often and that's enough for me. I have had them around for three years and when that part is over I'll be very glad.

—Stepmother, clerical worker

I'll tell you something embarrassing. If there's a type of man I'd like to marry it's his son [her husband's son]. He is only five years younger ... he is so warm, he's been good to his mother so that's a great sign ... I just fantasize about it, but I'd never do it.

—Stepmother, student

Studies of divorce and remarriage have largely neglected what it means to be a stepparent and how it affects one's life, especially one's marital life. It is only recently that researchers and research-oriented clinicians have focused on this topic, generally as part of studies on the entire reconstituted family system and, occasionally, as "how-to" books (Burgoyne and Clark 1984; Brown 1982; Jacobson 1979; Maddox 1975; Messinger 1976; Robinson 1980; Visher and Visher 1978). A majority of the published studies on stepkin relationships have placed a heavy emphasis on the experience of stepchildren, especially with their stepfathers (Bohannan 1975; Ferri 1984; Harper 1984; McCormick 1974; Perkins and Kahan 1979; Rallings 1976; Stern 1978). Fewer studies have focused on stepmothers (Bowerman and Irish 1962; Duberman 1973; Furstenberg 1987a, 1987b; Visher and Visher 1979), perhaps because only a minority of stepmothers live with their stepchildren (Glick 1980, 1984, 1989).[1]

At a time when the role of parent, and especially the maternal role, is being reconsidered, both at the personal and the social levels, it is only appropriate that more attention is finally being paid to stepparenting, especially when considering the higher divorce and remarriage rates and the fact that divorces include children more often than not. There are other reasons why the study of stepparenting is particularly topical and important. For instance, research is being done on the difficulties surrounding the maternal role (e.g., Boulton 1983) in a society which offers little support to mothers at the structural and economic levels. Similarly, the father role is receiving more attention in the literature (Klimmer and Kohl 1984; Lamb 1981; Levine et al. 1982; Lewis and Pleck 1979; McKee and O'Brien 1982; Russell 1983; Stein 1984). The decreasing birth rate of the past decade may be an indication that the parenting role is seen as costly. Many individuals limit their family size or chose to remain childless (Houseknecht 1979); yet, many of these same persons are faced with the consequently anomalous situation of becoming stepparents when they marry a person with children.

This chapter will focus first on the structural aspects of stepparenting. On the following page, I suggest important variables that should be studied in conjunction with the stepparenting experience. My sample size allows the study of only a few. There are three basic, although not exhaustive, structural stepparenting situations in terms of where the stepchildren are living: stepchildren live with stepparent; live with other parent; live on their own. Each of these living arrangements carries behavioral and attitudinal possibilities which have yet to be explored thoroughly (see also, Clingempeel et al. 1984, 1987).

Under current custody arrangements, more male stepparents experience a live-in stepchild while more female stepparents experience a visiting stepchild (Glick 1980). In a majority of the existing studies referred to earlier, structural situations are not adequately explored. For instance, it is not known if stepfathers who have visiting stepchildren are better accepted and accept their role better than stepfathers who have live-in stepchildren. On the female side, there are many indications that the role of stepmothers may be more difficult than that of stepfathers (Bowerman and Irish 1962; Burgoyne and Clark 1982a; Fishman and Hamel 1981; Guisinger et al. 1989), but it is not known how stepfathers and stepmothers compare under the two structural situations of visiting and live-in stepchildren (exc., see Duberman 1973). Unfortunately, obtaining a sufficiently large and representative sample of live-in stepmothers to compare with live-in stepfathers is very difficult because the former situation occurs only rarely.

Suggested Analytical Schema for the Stepparenting Experience

- Concurrent Structural Variables
  Location of Stepchildren
      Live with stepparent
      Live with other parent: they visit; they do not visit
      Live on their own: they visit; they do not visit
  Stepparent has no children from previous marriage
  Stepparent's children from previous marriage live with stepparent
  Stepparent's children from previous marriage live with their other parent
  Stepparent's children from previous marriage live on their own
  No children born to the remarriage
  Children born to the remarriage

- Additional Independent (Demographic) Variables*
  Stepparent's sex
  Stepchild's sex
  Stepparent's age at remarriage
  Stepparent's age at study time
  Stepchild's age at remarriage
  Stepchild's age at study time
  Stepparent's employment status (homemaker, employed for pay, unemployed)

Stepparent's socioeconomic status
Stepparent's previous marital status (single vs. divorced or
   widowed)
Number of stepchildren

Note: * Additional independent variables as suggested by each researcher's
   theoretical leanings and research interests

Another structural variable is whether the new marriage has
produced a child or children.[2] How does this affect the
stepparenting experience (Ganong and Coleman 1988)? Again,
this question can be answered fully only when considered in
relation to where the stepchildren live. More common, however,
is the third structural situation: whether or not the stepparents also
had children from a previous marriage and where those children
live. The most frequent occurrence is for men to have live-in
stepchildren while their own children live with their mother.
These men not only experience a disruption in the structure of
their paternal role, but are suddenly vested with a new set of
children who "belong" to their new wife. They have to devote some
time to their stepchildren (if only for the reason of their being
present), while they may resent not being able to see their own
children more often (see Duberman 1973; Messinger 1984). They
may have to support their live-in stepchildren *and* their children
and may suffer from many conflicts of loyalty (Clingempeel et al.
1987).

However, we would expect that live-in stepmothers who do not
have the custody of their own children will suffer from even more
conflicts because such women are often stigmatized in our society
(Duberman 1973, p. 287; Spanier and Thompson 1984, p. 78). In
addition, when women opt to leave their children in the custody
of their ex-husbands because they wish to be free from the daily
duties of their maternal role, they may not be so likely to remarry
custodial fathers. There is no literature documenting this directly;
however, in the current study, it is significant that not one
noncustodial mother remarried a custodial father. Moreover, only
one of these noncustodial mothers had children from her
remarriage and she clearly indicated that these children were to
compensate for the loss of her first ones: she had not chosen
noncustody and her ex-husband had manipulated the children

away from her psychologically. (This was corroborated during three interviews with the ex-husband since 1980.) Therefore, the statistical chance that such a double anomaly will occur in a remarriage (a non-custodial mother married to a custodial father) is slim and makes it even more problematic to study.

The purpose of this chapter is to examine the diversity and complexity of the structure of the stepparenting experience. Two key areas in the experience of stepparenting are examined: stepparents' reported marital life and their perceived relationship with their stepchildren. These two sets of dependent variables are studied in conjunction with stepchildren's locale of residence (live-in stepchildren, stepchildren living with other parent, and living on their own), and, more briefly, while considering where stepparents' children from a previous marriage live as well as the presence of children born to the remarriage. Also examined are stepsiblings' relationships as perceived by stepparents. Situations involving stepchildren will be compared with situations including no stepchildren, so as to see if the presence or absence of stepchildren affects the marital relationship. This comparison is extremely important in view of the finding that childless couples are happier than couples with children (Gove and Geerken 1977; Houseknecht 1979). A similar trend when no stepchildren exist could be expected.

A final focus of this chapter will be on the household division of labor: Do husbands and wives who have stepchildren adopt a more equalitarian division of labor? More specifically, when a woman acquires stepchildren, does her husband compensate for the surplus of work by doing more housework himself? Because many of the issues raised in the introduction to this chapter concerned potential gender differences, the analysis of the data is carried out along gender lines.

DATA COLLECTION

There were questions in the interviews that addressed the following demographic areas: whether a married person was a stepparent; where the stepchildren lived; whether there were children born from the remarriage; whether the stepparent was also a parent from a previous marriage; and where these children lived.

Several questions measuring the perceived quality of the respondents' marital relationship were included: marital happiness; satisfaction with spouse and perception of spouse's satisfaction with self. (These topics are discussed in Chapter IV.) Two related measures of the stepparenting experience consisted: (1) asking them if they would be "happier, less happy, or the same" if they did not have stepchildren and, (2) if they would get along with their spouse "better, less well, or not differently" without stepchildren. In a section dealing with potential sources of conflict between the spouses, one question dealt with conflicts engendered by one's stepchildren (spouses always agree about stepchildren = 1; always disagree = 5).

In addition, the interviews allowed me to explore the stepparents' feeling for their stepchildren; the stepparents' perception of how close their relationship was with their stepchildren and perceptions of their stepchildren's feelings towards them.[3] When the stepparents also were parents from a previous marriage, four questions focused on the interrelations of these two sets of children: How do they get along? How often do they quarrel? How do they feel about each other? Would their own children be happier without stepchildren?

In terms of the husband's input into household activities, six items were presented: Who *usually* does or is responsible for the (1) beds, (2) house cleaning, (3) paying the bills, (4) the laundry, (5) shopping for food, (6) and cooking? These six items were chosen over others (such as car washing) because they represented chores that have to be carried out in all homes, whether rich or poor, apartment located or in a large detached home, with children or no children, car or no car. However, because of this requisite, no questions were asked on the various aspects of child care.

There were 109 stepparents in the sample. In addition, 79 remarried or married respondents did not have stepchildren. In other words, this chapter focuses on respondents who were remarried or married for the first time to a formerly-divorced person. In some of these couples, only one spouse was a stepparent while in others both spouses were stepparents.

STEPPARENTS' MARITAL RELATIONSHIP

This section focuses only on the right-hand panel of Table VII.1. Only the one-way ANOVAS and chi-squares that were statistically significant are presented. (Two-way ANOVAS' main effect for residence were statistically significant when one-way ANOVAS by residence were for women.) Stepchildren's locale of residence was significantly related to six of the eight indicators of marital relationship for stepmothers. The results for stepfathers were nonsignificant and mixed in that some followed the direction of the results for stepmothers while others did not. Stepmothers who lived with their stepchildren reported a very high level of marital happiness and were totally satisfied with their spouse after an average of two years of remarriage. These stepmothers also believed that their husband was satisfied with them. The stepmothers who reported getting along best with their husband were these same stepmothers with live-in stepchildren.

In contrast, when stepchildren were relatively young and lived with the other parent, stepmothers were less happy maritally and had more conflicts with their husband. They neither felt appreciated by their husband nor did they appreciate him as much. While stepfathers were not as affected by stepchildren's locale of residence, for them the ideal situation was when the stepchildren were on their own. It is possible here that it was the *age* of the respondents or even of the stepchildren which created this small difference among stepfathers: stepchildren who were on their own were older and so were their stepfathers. The experience of having older stepchildren who are on their own has not been studied; the conversational data pointed to this situation as one potentially rich in terms of human relationships and in terms of the establishment of an extended kin system.

Nearly one-third of stepparents with live-in stepchildren but over half of those with stepchildren living with the other parent felt that they would get along better with their spouse without stepchildren and that their marriage would be happier. The conversational material presented expresses the stepparenting dilemma quite well. When the stepchildren lived with the other parent, the spouses felt much more that their marriage would be happier without these stepchildren who came in for disquieting visits and whose other parent often ruined the peace. However, men whose stepchildren lived with the other biological parent felt that they disagreed slightly less with their spouse about these stepchildren than when they lived with them.

Table VII.1. Respondent's Marital Relationship by Presence or Absence of Stepchildren, Stepchildren's Residence, and Gender of Stepparent

| | Presence or Absence of Stepchildren | | | | Stepchildren's Locale of Residence* | | | | | |
| | Respondents Do Not Have Stepchildren | | All Respondents with Stepchildren | | Stepchildren Live with Subject | | Stepchildren Live with other Parent | | Stepchildren Live on Own | |
Dependent Variables	Men (N=45)	Women (N=34)	Men (N=48)	Women (N=61)	Men (N=37)	Women (N=10)	Men (N=5)	Women (N=42)	Men (N=6)	Women (N=9)
1. Marital happiness 1 = high; 5 = low	1.76	1.56	1.33	1.85	1.32	1.20	1.40	2.00	1.33	1.89
2. Satisfaction with spouse 1 = high; 5 = low	1.60	1.62	1.29	2.02	1.32	1.00	1.20	2.26	1.17	2.00
3. Perception of spouse's satisfaction with self 1 = high; 5 = low	1.36	1.27	1.33	1.43	1.30	1.00	1.80	1.57	1.17	1.22
4. Getting along with spouse 1 = poor; 4 = well	2.96	3.03	3.17	2.93	3.13	3.50	3.00	2.71	3.50	3.33
5. Frequency of arguments with spouse 1 = many; 4 = none	2.84	2.86	3.00	2.79	2.92	3.30	2.80	2.60	3.67	3.11
6. Agreement with spouse's children 1 = always agree; 5 = never agree					1.81	1.90	1.60	2.29	1.33	1.78

7. Would marriage be happier without stepchildren	22%	30%	60%	54%	20%	22%
8. If there were no stepchildren would get along with spouse better	30%	30%	40%	40%	20%	22%

Notes: ANOVAs are only for locale of residence:

1. One-way ANOVA for women: $F = 2.485$, $p < .092$
2. Two-way ANOVA: for interaction: $F = 3.07$, $p < .051$
   One-way ANOVA for women: $F = 4.050$, $p < .023$
3. One-way ANOVA for women: $F = 3.453$, $p < .038$
4. One-way ANOVA for women: $F = 3.643$, $p < .032$
5. One-way ANOVA for women: $F = 3.153$, $p < .050$
6. N.S.
7. Chi-square for women $= 11.2075$, 4 df, $p < .024$
8. N.S.

The following is a summary of what transpired in the conversational segments of the interviews. While it was not generally easy for either a man or a woman to raise, support, and care for live-in stepchildren, the live-in situation was felt to be a less divisive one than when the children lived with the other parent and came for visits. In the former situation, the new couples mentioned that they had more control, were less at the mercy of the ex-spouses, and the stepchildren became part of the household rather than occasional and at times disruptive guests. Moreover, when fathers had custody and remarried, a great deal more planning was reportedly done to ensure the stability of the unit than if they did not have custody. This stems in part from the anomaly of the situation in terms of its rarity. This anomaly also led wives to feel more "appreciated" because they contributed to raising their *husband's* children. They knew that the situation was unusual in that few divorced men have custody of their children. These wives felt closer to their husband and feared the ex-wife's influence and criticism much less than if their husband's children were with the ex-wife. The new wives unavoidably compared themselves to the ex-wives and felt superior. The husband's negative appraisal of the children's mother reflected well on the live-in stepmother. In spite of these advantages, and in spite of their high scores in Table VII.1, stepmothers also reflected a great deal of ambivalence about having live-in stepchildren as will be shown in a subsequent section.

THE MARITAL RELATIONSHIP: NONSTEPPARENTS VERSUS STEPPARENTS

One third of all stepparents felt that their marriage would be happier if they did not have stepchildren. When compared with those married and remarried respondents who did not have stepchildren, mixed results were obtained. Women who did not have stepchildren definitely assessed their marital happiness more positively than stepmothers. *But* their marital happiness was lower than that of the 10 stepmothers with live-in stepchildren. Men, in contrast, were happier maritally when they had stepchildren. Satisfaction with spouse followed the same differential results for men and women. However, there were no differences between stepparents and nonstepparents in terms of perception of spouse's satisfaction with self, although, once again women tended to be more positive without stepchildren (see left-hand panel of Table VII.1).

On the two measures of conflict, the differences were not statistically significant but, nevertheless, the same trends are encountered for the fourth indicator. Neither were there significant differences in terms of frequency of arguments.

Overall, stepmothers were less happy than nonstepmothers while the reverse generally occurred among men. Such results definitely indicate a problematic situation insofar as stepmothers are concerned in terms of their marital relationship. Moreover, well over one-third of all stepmothers felt that they would have a happier relationship without stepchildren, including those 10 live-in stepmothers who had near perfect scores of marital happiness. These results definitely indicate that *a marriage that brings in stepchildren may be more fragile than one without stepchildren even though marital happiness may be high.*

THE MARITAL RELATIONSHIP: PARENTS AND STEPPARENTS

I then went one step further and tried to see how a combination of having children from a previous marriage *and* having stepchildren affected the marital relationship. Although some of the frequencies are small, the results are interesting. If we look at the figures for each gender separately, we see that those women who assess their current marital happiness the most negatively have children from a previous marriage *and* stepchildren: they are mothers and stepmothers. For women, all in all, having children *or* stepchildren lowered their marital happiness. The optimal situation consisted in having neither type of children or in having no stepchildren but only children from the previous marriage. Actually, for women, the optimal situation in terms of marital happiness resided in having live-in stepchildren (1.20) or in having a new child from the remarriage (1.25). However, in this sample, women with "new" children tended not to have either stepchildren or children from their previous marriage, and the "new" children were all infants and preschoolers.

Table VII.2. Repondent's Perception of Their Situation by Presence (Or Absence) of Children from Previous Marriage and Presence (Or Absence) of Stepchildren

	No Children from Previous Marriage and No Stepchildren		Children From Previous Marriage and Stepchildren		Children From Previous Marriage but No Stepchildren		No Children From Previous Marriage but Stepchildren	
	Men (N=11)	Women (N=14)	Men (N=32)	Women (N=31)	Men (N=27)	Women (N=16)	Men (N=13)	Women (N=18)
Marital happiness 1 = high; 5 = low	1.91	1.57	1.44	2.00	1.89	1.56	1.15	1.67
Satisfaction with spouse	1.73	1.57	1.34	2.13	1.70	1.63	1.23	1.78
Perception of spouse's satisfaction with self	1.55	1.36	1.44	1.49	1.37	1.13	1.08	1.28
Getting along with spouse 1 = poor; 4 = well	2.55	3.14	3.09	2.94	2.96	3.13	3.31	3.06
Frequency of arguments with spouse 1 = many; 4 = none	2.55	2.79	2.97	2.84	2.81	3.06	3.00	2.78

For men, the highest level of marital happiness was reported by men who had no children from their previous marriage but had stepchildren (Table VII.2). The lowest level was reported by childless men with no stepchildren, the complete reverse of the findings for women.

The results for the variable of satisfaction with spouse followed those for marital happiness. In terms of perception of spouse's satisfaction for self, the results were more mixed, but again we see the importance of having stepchildren for men (and no children from previous marriage) and, for women, in not having stepchildren. These results again are related to the fact that most women who have stepchildren have visiting stepchildren while most men who have stepchildren have live-in stepchildren.

Men who got along best with their wife had stepchildren but no children of their own, while women were affected only in the fifth indicator (arguments). It is striking that, on all five indicators, the men with the worse scores had neither children nor stepchildren. And, still for men, having children from the previous marriage and no stepchildren was the second worse alternative.

FEELINGS FOR STEPCHILDREN

As shown in Table VII.3, both stepmothers and stepfathers developed a closer and deeper relationship with their live-in stepchildren than with stepchildren living elsewhere. While stepchildren's locale of residence was not related to stepfathers' marital life, it was related to their feelings toward their stepchildren. Despite the higher positive scores of live-in stepmothers shown in Tables VII.1 and VII.3 , these women were nonetheless ambivalent toward their live-in stepchildren, as expressed in the following qualitative material.

> [One stepmother reporting liking her stepson] I would choose him if I were asked to choose a stepson. He's a nice boy, very nice, mannered, not difficult. But I find it hard to take care of another woman's son and I have to keep telling myself that he is my husband's son. I don't think it's fair because she never babysits for me and I always do for her. She likes her freedom but it seems to me that she's having it at our expense. After the birth of our first

Table VII.3. Stepparents' Relationship with Stepchildren by Stepchildren's Residence and Stepparents' Gender

Stepparents' Relationship With Stepchildren	Stepchildren Living With Subject		Stepchildren Living With Other Parent		Stepchildren Living Living On Own	
	Men (N = 37)	Women (N = 10)	Men (N = 5)	Women (N = 43)	Men (N = 6)	Women (N = 9)
1. Closeness of relationship with stepchildren: 0 = very close; 8 = no contact	1.21	1.00	4.60	4.61	4.00	2.11
2. Feelings about stepchildren: 0 = very close; 8 = no contact	0.68	0.80	3.60	2.71	1.60	1.67
3. Perceived stepchildren's feelings about self: 0 = very close; 8 = no contact	1.08	0.90	3.80	3.13	2.60	2.67

Notes:
1. One-way ANVOA for men: F = 9.327, p < .000.
   One-way ANVOA for women: F = 11.212, p < .000.
2. One-way ANVOA for men: F = 13.352, p < .000.
   One-way ANVOA for women: F = 4.173, p < .021.
3. One-way ANVOA for men: F = 5.609, p < .007.
   One-way ANVOA for women: F = 4.868, p < .011.

138

child my husband told her that ... her son's weekends would have
to be more regular because I needed the rest with the baby. I think
they worked it out but you see it is a problem to care for a stepchild.
There are inequities involved and I am not sure I like being at the
receiving end.

This theme of inequity recurred throughout the interviews with
live-in stepmothers.

Yes, I feel it's not fair to have to keep someone else's children in
general. They're not related to me in any way by blood. If my
husband was widowed it would be different because I could become
their mother.

I'd rather not have my stepsons. Mind you, I care for them and I
am attached to them but I never set out to have children, and having
someone else's children is a burden. I often resent it. At the same
time, I wish they didn't have their mother so that way I would
benefit at least from being a mother. But in my situation I have
all the problems a mother has since they live here and none of the
advantages, may be less so with the younger one because he was
so little when I moved in.

It was also noticeable in the conversational parts of the
interviews that stepfathers with live-in stepchildren talked about
them much less than did similar stepmothers, probably a reflection
of the fact that stepmothers spent more time in close proximity
to their live-in stepchildren and took care of them more than did
stepfathers with live-in stepchildren. When stepfathers talked
about their live-in stepchildren, it was generally in relation to the
conflicts of loyalty vis-à-vis their biological children who did not
live with them:

So long as you have stepchildren you might as well have them with
you otherwise it's too complicated. It would be more simple if I had
my daughters here all the time. Visiting is a very complicated
arrangement both for parents and children. However, I would have
preferred not to have acquired stepdaughters. They're cute little girls.
The only problem is that my own daughters are jealous of them but
I think that it is getting better. I should adopt them but I feel I can't
do it so long as my own daughters don't live with me. So that part
is dicey.

However, men and women were equally verbose on the topic of stepchildren living with the *other* parent. The volume itself of conversational material gathered on this topic indicated the complexity of the situation. The following is a quote from a woman reminiscing about the problems created by visiting stepchildren in her previous remarriage:

> His kids kept coming here because he didn't want to visit them at their place, of course, because he hated his ex-wife. We had six kids here at times and his are the rough type: after they'd gone, the whole house was a mess for us to clean and the frig was empty and *I* had to pay. They were just low class persons in a bad sense.

Therefore, although live-in stepchildren were preferable to stepchildren living with the other parent, stepchildren were nevertheless a mixed blessing for stepparents, especially stepmothers. Stepparenting was a rewarding affective experience when it worked. But it was often considered to be an exploitative condition, at best a tolerated one. Stepparenting was a more difficult role for women in this sample because most women had stepchildren who lived with the "other woman," and it has been shown that, in this sample, it was the least favorable condition for stepmothers.

STEPCHILDREN AND OWN CHILDREN
FROM PREVIOUS MARRIAGE

This section and the next are presented more as a source of hypotheses for larger studies than as conclusive data. The following is a summary of the conversational material.

Both men and women felt that their own children and their stepchildren were more attached to each other and were getting along better when both sets of children were living together. However, there were only six such occurrences for whom all relevant data were gathered and these happened to be particularly successful remarriages.[5] In these six cases, with both sets of stepchildren living-in, the strength of the spousal relationship may have cemented the entire family. It is interesting to note that, in all six cases of an amalgamated family, the wives were not employed. In two cases, a custodial mother had remarried a widowed man. All in all, cases of amalgamated families were few probably because custodial fathers are few and often remarry a single, thus childless, woman.

In contrast, where women were custodial mothers and had stepchildren who lived with the other parent, the two sets of children were described as getting along less well and being less attached to each other than when living together. "They [daughters] don't get along well with my stepdaughters because there is too much jealousy, and when these girls [visiting stepdaughters] get here they want their father all to themselves and my little girls have difficulty coping with this." However, there were no noncustodial women with live-in stepchildren and, conversely, there were no custodial fathers whose stepchildren lived with their own fathers. We were, therefore, unable to test for possible gender combinations of stepparents and parents in this area.

Along the same lines of attachment, stepfathers were more attached to their live-in stepchildren when their own children lived with them than when their children lived with the other parent. For a man, at least, having custody of one's own children increased his chances of a close relationship with live-in stepchildren. When a man's children lived with their mother, but his stepchildren lived with him, he was drawn to his stepchildren when he had no access to own children or when they had sorely disappointed him. But when he had access to them, however limited the access was (either by himself or by the other parent), he maintained a certain distance with live-in stepchildren as if fearing to be unfair to own children by giving affection to his wife's children.

STEPCHILDREN AND NEW CHILDREN

What happens to the stepparent's feelings toward stepchildren with the arrival of a child or children in the remarriage? Although there were 25 remarriages with at least one "new" child, the cell sizes for "new" children were limited for the purpose of statistical analysis, not only because most of the children had been born to persons previously childless, but also because I was subdividing them by the place of residence of stepchildren, as well as by the presence of own children from a previous marriage. There were few cases of respondents with live-in stepchildren *and* children from the new marriage, and only one man had live-out stepchildren and children from his new marriage. (In other words only one noncustodial mother had children in her remarriage: her case has been previously discussed.)

The qualitative and quantitative material indicated that the five men who had live-in stepchildren and a child from the new marriage were, not only the happiest maritally, but also those stepfathers with the warmest feelings toward their stepchildren. "The baby has provided me with a secure feeling; he is the symbol of family life. My wife's daughter [live-in] is a very pleasant child who needs a father and she is a sharp contrast to my [older, visiting] daughter. These two children have healed the wounds ... we have children of our own, not a child here and a child there and no custody problems." In contrast, the three women who had live-in stepchildren and a child from the new marriage, although very happy maritally, were significantly more distant from their live-in stepchildren than *all* other categories of stepmothers with live-in stepchildren. These three women would have wanted to devote more of themselves to the child born of this marriage and less to the children born during the husband's previous marriage. "I think I am less patient with them [live-in stepchildren] since he's born. He is *mine* and they're not, but they're always here and I just don't seem to be able to be alone with the baby, you know to get to be a *mother*. I'd like that so much but these children are in the way. They have a mother and they don't belong to *this* marriage." It is important to note that these three mothers were primaparous. They might have felt differently had they had children from a previous marriage.

HOUSEHOLD DIVISION OF LABOR

One element that has not been explored in the literature and was of interest to me is whether a man increases his contribution to the household and childcare labor when he brings children to his new wife (Fishman and Hamel 1981). Does a live-in stepmother benefit from a greater housework contribution from her husband than does a woman whose stepchildren do not live with her? The equity aspect of exchange theory (Blau 1964) would lead us to expect this to occur because the stepchild(ren) can be seen as a surplus of labor for the wife and, in order to compensate, the husband may raise his share of household and childcare duties. Does a stepmother who receives visiting stepchildren but has no children of her own or has children from the new marriage only also obtain the same benefit? Here again, one would expect it to be so because that stepmother has to care, at least temporarily, for her *husband's* children while he does not have to do the same for her—assuming he does not have to support them.

I have described the six questions pertaining to the division of labor in the Data Gathering section. There were several options: self, wife or husband, children, paid help, the entire family, no one in particular, self and spouse. In order to be entered in Table VII.4, anyone of these options had to have received at least 15% of the mentions, so as to reduce the size of the Table. Husbands and wives agreed within each couple in 72% of the cases. This reasonably high level of agreement is reflected in Table VII.4. The cases of disagreement were generally caused by husbands who answered "self and wife" while their wives answered that they themselves did these chores. Husbands attributed to themselves a greater share of the work then their wives attributed to them. Husbands, however, agreed that wives were doing these chores more often than not.

In summary, the results of Table VII.4 do not support any principle of equity: women who had to care for live-in stepchildren were no more likely to benefit from their husbands' "help" than were women who did not have stepchildren or whose stepchildren visited. In fact, the most equalitarian couples were found among those formed by a relatively young woman remarried to a man previously single, often a man younger than she. These women were by no means in an equalitarian situation but meal preparation and grocery shopping tended to be done jointly or serially by one or the other more often than in the other cases in the study.

Observations during the interviews and analysis of the conversational material clearly indicated that live-in stepchildren were cared for by their live-in stepmother rather than father, as were a woman's own live-in children. When stepchildren visited, stepmothers acted as hostesses, cooks, and laundresses while these

Table VII.4. Division of Labor by Presence of Stepchildren, Stepchildren's Residence, and Stepparents' Gender

	Respondents Without Stepchildren		Respondents With Stepchildren		Stepchildren Living With Respondent		Stepchildren Living With Other Parent	
	Men (N = 44)	Women (N = 35)	Men (N = 40)	Women (N = 50)	Men (N = 35)	Women (N = 10)	Men (N = 5)	Women (N = 40)
Who makes the beds	no one / paid help / wife	no one / self	no one* / paid help	paid help / paid help* / self	no one / wife	paid help / family	no one / paid help	paid help / no one / self
Who cleans the house	paid help / wife	paid help / self / no one	paid help / family / wife / no one	paid help*	paid help	paid help*	paid help* / no one	paid help* / self
Who pays the bills	self* / wife	husband* / self	wife* / self	self* / husband	wife* / self	husband* / self	wife* / self	self* / husband
Who does the laundry	wife* / paid help	self* / paid help	wife* / paid help / no one	paid help / self	wife* / paid help	self* / paid help	paid help* / no one	paid help / self
Who cooks the meals	wife / paid help / self and wife	self / self and husband	wife / self and wife	self / paid help	wife / self and wife	self / paid help	wife* / all family*	self* / paid help
Who shops for food	wife* / paid help	self* / self and husband	wife* / self and wife	self* / self and husband	wife* / self* / wife	self* / self and husband	self and wife* / wife	self / paid help

Note: * A person or a category of persons who have received 50% or more of the mentions.

144

children's fathers enjoyed the children's visits or, frequently, took them out. Thus, when the visits took place at home, stepmothers had additional work to do and many resented this. When the fathers took the children out, stepmothers were often left at home and excluded from that familial sub-unit.

DISCUSSION

The results clearly indicated that the stepparenting experience was a more positive one with live-in than live-out stepchildren. Both stepmothers and stepfathers were closer to their live-in stepchildren than other stepparents. However, even with live-in stepchildren, a great deal of ambivalence about stepparenting was expressed by stepmothers (Hobart 1988). The results also indicated that, after an average of two years of remarriage, *the perceived quality of stepmothers' marital life was significantly affected by the place of residence of stepchildren:* stepmothers with live-in stepchildren were most positive, while stepmothers whose stepchildren lived with their own mothers were the least positive in terms of their marital life. In contrast, stepfathers' perception of their marital life was not significantly affected by the variable under consideration. Nevertheless, from 20 to 60% of both stepmothers and stepfathers indicated that their marriage would be happier and more harmonious without stepchildren. These data would buttress White and Booth's findings (1985) that the presence of stepchildren negatively affects the stability of a remarriage.

To this I would venture that, *from a man's point of view, the destabilizing circumstance is the fact that his children are generally not living with him.* Therefore, when he has stepchildren, these children are a constant reminder of the fact that he cannot care for his own children. *From a woman's point of view, the destabilizing circumstance simply lies in the presence of children,* both hers and his—especially when his live elsewhere. *The combination of the mother and the stepmother roles was particularly detrimental;* however, becoming a mother within the new marriage was a positive experience. Men who had stepchildren but no children from a previous marriage were especially happy: they did not suffer from the absence of their own children while at the same time they generally developed a good relationship with their stepchildren whose own fathers were often neglectful, distant, or even absent.

The statistical data as well as the conversational material presented in this chapter also lend support to other researchers who have indicated that the role of stepmother is a more difficult one than that of stepfather (Burgoyne and Clark 1982; Duberman 1973; Fishman and Hamel 1981; Furstenburg 1987). On the basis of our structural analysis, we can go one step further and hypothesize that the greater difficulty and complexity of the stepmother role may stem from the fact that most stepmothers do not have live-in stepchildren—which was the most favorable structural variable in this study from the stepmothers' perspective (but not from that of *stepchildren* in Furstenberg and Nord's [1985] study). In contrast, most stepfathers have live-in stepchildren. A second explanation may reside in that *it is generally the stepmothers, and not the stepfathers, who are responsible for childcare and household functioning* (see Santrock and Sitterle 1987).

When stepchildren visited, the stepmothers, and *not* their fathers, inherited additional work (house cleaning, cooking, food shopping, bedmaking) and this work was perceived as a burden because stepmothers benefited little emotionally from the visits. However, with live-in stepchildren, although additional work also befell the women, they at least felt attached to their stepchildren and felt that the latter returned the attachment. The live-in stepchildren did more household chores as well to help their stepmother. These stepmothers felt more secure than the ones whose husband had to visit his children and cater to his ex-wife, whether financially or in terms of childcare help (Visher and Visher 1979). When the stepchildren lived with them, stepmothers felt they were raising them and were part of a team with their husband (Furstenberg and Spanier 1984). In the visiting situation, stepmothers felt left out because their husband's coparental role was carried out more with the ex-wife than with them. *The husbands' coparental role was threatening to the new wives' sense of security as they feared a renewed emotional bond between their husband and the ex-wife.* This insecurity stems in part from the fact that we lack clear-cut norms separating the ex-spouses' coparental role from emotional bonding (see Ahrons 1980, 1979; McGoldrick and Carter 1980).[6]

In the routine of daily contacts, stepchildren and stepparents developed a closer relationship; quarrels were more easily overshadowed by other pleasant daily occurrences. With visiting stepchildren, a quarrel stood out as the event of the week; ill feelings simmered without opportunities for healing during the hob-nob of daily activities and were often exacerbated by the children's mother's own comments. Moreover, *fathers were more likely to side with their children when they were visiting,* leaving the stepmothers feeling bruised, *while fathers were more likely to form a coalition with their new wife with live-in children* (and stepchildren).

Similarly, as in Duberman's study (1975), there were indications that own children and stepchildren got along better when they lived together most of the time than when one set merely visited the house of the other. The rationale for this would follow the same line as that already delineated for the stepparents.

It has also been shown that a combination of live-in own children and stepchildren was positive for both stepmothers and stepfathers, but that the combination of live-in stepchildren and new children from *current* marriage was less favorable for the stepmothers/live-in stepchildren relationships.[7] Although the frequencies are so limited that no conclusions are drawn, these latter data are nevertheless interesting because women who had children from a *previous* marriage and live-in stepchildren were the most attached stepmothers. The implication was that both sets of children were from a *previous* marriage and had a similar meaning to the women. These children represented the past and were equal. In comparison, the children or child issued to the *current* marriage had a special meaning: they represented the present. In addition, these women did not have a child from a previous marriage: the "new" children were their first and only children. Generally, the stepparenting experience has already begun before the baby arrives: the baby modifies this experience as the stepparent becomes a parent. The addition of this role may bring a contrast in the way the parenting and stepparenting roles are played, while no such a comparison may have been made before the baby's arrival. It is also possible that these women may have made a clearer distinction between their stepparental and parental roles (Visher and Visher 1979).

Men may have an easier time accepting live-in stepchildren after their wife has given them a child, while women who bear, nurse, and care for their new child may feel that the live-in stepchildren intrude in their intimacy with their own biological child. But there were also indications that the new child made stepmothers tolerate visiting stepchildren better. Here, it might be hypothesized that, with the arrival of the new child, stepmothers feel that they finally are on a team with their husband and may be less threatened by the visiting stepchildren and their mother. Duberman (1975) also found that a new child often contributed to the integration of the reconstituted family. More recently, White et al. (1985) have found that a new child increases a live-in stepchild's attachment to his/her stepfather, even to the detriment of the noncustodial father.

Both the statistical analyses carried out for this chapter and the conversational material presented suggest the breadth of research on stepparenting that has yet to be undertaken. Other variables which should be considered are the time elapsed since remarriage, the age of the stepparents and stepchildren at remarriage, the number and gender of stepchildren, stepparents' socioeconomic status and previous marital status. Because of this multiplicity of relevant variables, large samples will be required for statistical analyses. However, qualitative and semi-qualitative studies may prove equally fruitful in studying the processes involved and in discovering those questions which would be meaningful to explore further (LaRossa and Wolf 1980; Sprey 1985).

The parenting experience is generally, although by no means always, a chosen fate. In contrast, one does not generally choose to become a stepparent or even wish to become a stepparent: it is a condition which "happens" as a result of forming a relationship with a previously-married person. It is also a situation which seems to carry a different set of consequences for men and women and is *more detrimental to women, specially when they have to combine maternal and stepmaternal roles.* The data on the division of labor may offer one explanation for this detrimental gender difference: *stepmothers acquire more household servitude.* Because a great proportion of the stepmothers in this study were employed (many had careers), the addition of the stepparenting role to their already crowded lives could only be problematic in a society which already offers so few support systems to mothers and, consequently, to stepmothers.

NOTES

1.   Comparisons of relationships and attitudes in stepfather and natural father families have also been made (Perkins and Kahan 1979; Santrock et al. 1982; Wilson et al. 1975).

2.   Duberman's work (1973, 1975) has been especially inspiring in devising the structural orientation of the present chapter. Another important topic not herein covered is the stepgrandparenting-stepgrandchildren relationship (Sanders and Trygstad 1989).

3.   These questions were operationalized as follows: "How do you feel about your stepchildren? Love them, like them a lot, like them some, do not like them, resent them? How would you describe your relationship with your stepchildren? Very close, fairly close, not too close, not close at all, no contact. And do you know how they feel about you? Love us ... I don't know." The coding took into account those respondents who liked one stepchild but disliked the other, for instance. Thus, in Table VII.2, love them = 0; like them a lot = 1; like them some = 3; love/like some but not others = 4 .... to dislike them = 7, and no contact = 8.

4.   "On their own" included married stepchildren or others old enough to live independently, as well as three cases of adolescents residing in group homes.

5.   In three cases, the amalgamation was not total in that one of the two spouses had only one child from the previous marriage at home while the other child(ren) was (were) living with the ex-spouuse.

6.   On the lack of institutionalization of the stepparental role in general, see Cherlin (1978), Fast and Cain (1966) Visher and Visher (1982).

7.   The sample did not have a situation involving live-in own children, live-in stepchildren, and "new" children or, if you wish, the romanticized "yours, mine, and ours" situation under one roof.

Chapter VIII

The Divorce/Remarriage Chains

My wife and my ex-wife have started a babysitting program. We owe them two points already.

Personally, I don't have anything to do with him [wife's ex-husband]. He never bothers me whereas my ex-wife does not mind calling my wife to ask her for advice. If we would let her do it, she'd soon have my wife as her new mother.

It does feel like a family, a large one .. we [the new couple and their exes] have seven children and they all get along. Once in a while their daughters [from the remarriage] bike up to our house and visit for a while. They're used to having my daughters over and they see their brother coming here so they must think this is a second home.

I would say that our only problem is lack of time for all the commitments we have. I wish we didn't have to see all these exes and their wives or husbands and their stepchildren. There's no privacy. My wife feels especially burdened with all these, these constraining relationships that normal families do not have to deal with.

My son is in contact with a very large family. He has two half brothers and occasionally he sees my ex-husband's wife's children and they become like cousins in the long run because they know they will always run into each other or be included in small family reunions.

We don't socialize. It's strictly business for the children's sake. I didn't marry my husband to acquire his ex-wife or her new husband, and my husband certainly does not want to be saddled with my ex-

151

> *husband and his girlfriend. No. These relationships are nice on a TV screen but not in real life.*

Various aspects of the relationship between former spouses and between the spouses of a remarriage have been examined in great detail. This chapter takes relationships created by divorce and remarriage one step further and extends this inquiry to the network. Divorce and remarriage create the potential for additional relationships: new spouses, new sets of in-laws or affines, and stepchildren (Whiteside 1989). In this chapter, we ask: When a woman marries a formerly-divorced man, what kind of a relationship does she have with *his* ex-wife? Respondents talked of their "husband's ex," or their "wife's ex-husband" or their "wife's former husband." On the other hand, what kind of a relationship does a man have with his ex-wife's new husband? Respondents mentioned their "ex-wife's husband" or their "former wife's new husband" or their "ex-husband's wife."

What is striking in these concepts is the very primitive terminology: it consists of "exes" or "former" hyphenated with "husband" or "wife" with the addition of one more "husband" or "wife" as appropriate. Thus, a cluster of nouns and adjectives is used to refer to a quasi-kin relationship in some cases, and in most other cases a relationship created by legal situations, that is, divorce and remarriage. These concept clusters do not convey any affective content: we do not know how cordial or embattled the relationships are. It is obvious that the English language yet has to develop a more accurate and meaningful set of words to reflect these social realities.

Divorce and remarriage introduce *chains* of persons currently married to each other or previously married to each other and their own spouses or former spouses. A chain is shown on the following page.

Outside the married pairs (solid lines) there is very little interaction. Male B does not have a relationship with Male A who is his wife's ex-husband. Neither does Male C have any relationship with Male B who is also his wife's ex-husband. Finally, Female A does not have a relationship with Female B who is her husband's ex-wife. Only Females B and C interact on rare occasions, perhaps because Male C has maintained cordial feelings for his ex-wife. Essentially, these people form a legal chain rather than a network.

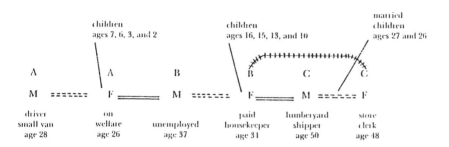

However, the next diagram has have elements of a network. In order to simplify the comparison, I have chosen another chain consisting of two married couples, as was the previous case. This is a network. First, Female B has a relationship with Female A who is her husband's ex-wife. Female B also has a relationship with Female C who is her ex-husband's new wife. In addition, Males A and B also have a relationship, albeit distant or aloof. (Females A and C do not interact, however, as they belong to the two extremes of the network. There were occasional networks in which such relationships have been formed.)

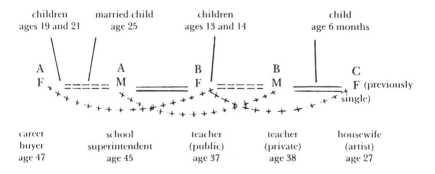

These two diagrams introduce the three topics of this chapter:

- a person's relationship with spouse's ex-spouse;
- a person's relationship with ex-spouse's new spouse;
- relationships between these various persons or lack of such relationship: networks versus chains.

Although Bohannan (1971) has detailed a few interesting cases of persons who had developed a friendship with their new spouse's ex-husband/wife, we have very little concrete information on this matter, as is indicated by the paucity of references on this topic (Goetting 1980). It is possible that the more "intriguing," thus unusual, cases are the ones heard of or recalled when gathering impressionistic data on a subject. These cases might be hardly representative and a more systematic inquiry is necessary.

There is even less information in the literature on the relationship with a person's ex-spouse's new spouse. This may stem in part from the fact that well over one-third of all ex-spouses do not stay in touch, as was illustrated in Chapter III. Such a situation reduces the possibility of a relationship with the ex-spouse's new spouse. Moreover, the emphasis in research has been more on the ex-spousal relationship than on any further quasi-kin ramifications.

RELATIONSHIP WITH SPOUSE'S EX-SPOUSE

The respondents included in this section were the 163 remarried persons as well as the 34 persons married for the first time to a previously divorced individual. The indicators for a person's relationship with the spouse's ex-spouse are divided into three categories. First, indicators of the frequency of interaction with spouse's ex: how often the ex is seen; how often respondent talks to spouse's ex over the phone. Second, indicators of the quality of the relationship included how respondent defines relationship with spouse's ex, and feelings toward spouse's ex; then, how respondent perceives spouse's ex's feelings toward self, and whether or not respondent sees spouse's ex as interfering in the new marriage. A third category of indicators pertains to how the spouse's ex affects the respondent and his/her spouse's level of agreement.

Table VIII.1. Respondents' Relationship with Spouse's Ex-Spouse: Levels of Significance

	Respondent's Gender	Respondent's Marital Status Married vs. Remarried	New Spouse's Children From Previous Marriage	Where the Stepchildren Live	Respondent's Employment Status	Spouse's ex's Marital Status Remarried vs. Unmarried
How often respondent sees spouse's ex	N.S.	N.S.	$p < .0001$	$p < .0697$	N.S.	Trend
How often respondent talks to spouse's ex	$p < .0723$	N.S.	$p < .0001$	N.S.	N.S.	N.S.
Respondent's perceived quality of relationship with spouse's ex	$p < .0832$	N.S.	$p < .0001$	$p < .0316$	N.S.	N.S.
Respondent's feelings for spouse's ex	N.S.	Trend	$p < .012$	N.S.	N.S.	N.S.
Respondent's perception of spouse's ex's feeling for self	N.S.	N.S.	$p < .0001$	N.S.	N.S.	N.S.
Respondent's perception of spouse's ex's interference in own marriage	N.S.	N.S.	$p < .0002$	N.S.	N.S.	Trend
Repondent's perceived agreement with spouse about spouse's ex	N.S.	N.S.	$p < .0018$	Trend	Trend	N.S.

155

Nearly 46% of the respondents reported never seeing their spouse's ex. In all, 64% reported no real relationship. These results are relatively skewed in the direction of a very low level of interaction between a person and his or her spouse's ex-spouse.

I had expected that there might be some variation in this relationship along the independent variables listed on the top of Table VIII.1. For instance, in view of the younger ages of married women compared to remarried women in this sample, it seemed logical that a woman in a first marriage might be more intimidated by her husband's first wife than a woman who is herself an ex-spouse. I had also hypothesized that an employed person would be better disposed toward a spouse's ex than one who is unemployed because the employed person has an alternative source of satisfaction. The other variables in Table VIII.1 are self-explanatory.

Only the levels of significance are presented in Table VIII.1. Therefore the comparative percentages will be detailed. If the order of the independent variables listed in Table VIII.1 is followed, gender attracts immediate attention. Women reported being in touch verbally with the spouse's ex on a regular basis more often than males: 16% of the men versus 32% of the women. The two women (wife and ex-wife) communicated more than the two men (husband and ex-husband). Then, women respondents described their relationship with the spouse's ex as being friendly (31% vs. 21% for men) *and* unfriendly (11% vs. 3% for men) more frequently, while men overwhelmingly described it as nonexistent (76%)—which explains why the two men do not talk over the phone, for instance. Men and women, however, gave similar responses for the other variables.

When the respondents were remarried (the next variable), they tended to say that they liked the spouse's ex more often than was the case when the respondents were in a first marriage (24% vs. 9%). The married respondents tended to declare themselves neutral (72%) more often than the remarried (56%). Otherwise, current marital status made little difference, contrary to what I had hypothesized.

Whether or not the new spouse had children from a previous marriage was consistently and significantly related to a difference on all the dependent variables. This is well in accordance with the results obtained in Chapter III for the relationship between ex-spouses. When stepchildren existed, respondents more often reported seeing the spouse's ex regularly than when there were no stepchildren (37% vs. 4%). In fact, 88% of the respondents without stepchildren reported never seeing the spouse's ex. The same held for telephone conversations: without stepchildren, 90% never held a conversation over the phone with the spouse's ex. The same applied to the perceived quality of the relationship: 35% of the respondents with stepchildren described it as friendly, 11%, as unfriendly and 54% as nonexistent. In contrast, without stepchildren, 92% felt that there was no relationship at all and only 8% believed it to be friendly. No one without stepchildren mentioned an unfriendly relationship because without stepchildren and thus without the necessity of being in touch with the spouse's ex, a potentially unfriendly situation rapidly turned into a no-relationship situation. Respondents with stepchildren were as likely to have positive (26%) as negative (22%) feelings toward the spouse's ex, while 52% felt neutral (versus 78% of those without stepchildren). The same applied for the perception of the spouse's ex's feelings for the respondent: 25% positive, 25% negative, only 9% neutral with stepchildren. Another 45% said that they did not know how the person felt about them while 88% of those without stepchildren chose this alternative.

Few respondents actually felt that the spouse's ex interfered in their marriage but all those who did had stepchildren, as would be expected from the previous results: 13% said that the spouse's ex intruded sometimes, and 18% said rarely while the rest said never. No one chose the "often" alternative. Finally, when there were stepchildren, the respondents agreed less with their spouse about the spouse's ex than was the case without stepchildren (1.4 vs. 1.0). In spite of this difference, the level of agreement on this item was nevertheless very high as total disagreement would have brought a score of 5.0.

The analysis of the stepparenting experience in Chapter VI indicated that the stepchildren's place of residence was a crucial variable. However, this variable is not as crucial here as is the mere presence of stepchildren. When the children lived with the stepparent, the stepparent reported seeing the spouse's ex on a regular basis more often than when the stepchildren lived elsewhere: 27% versus 4%. Perhaps unexpectedly, therefore, with live-in stepchildren, the respondents tended to reveal that no relationship with the spouse's ex existed in 65% of the cases (while those with stepchildren living elsewhere reported no relationship in only 46% of the cases). Two respondents who had frequent phone contacts with the spouse's ex insisted that no relationship existed as it was the spouse's ex who was always phoning; they felt they had nothing to do with it. With live-in stepchildren, the spouse's ex was more often *seen* but this did not necessarily imply that a *relationship* existed.

It is obvious that the spouse's ex is not overly popular among the wives and husbands. Even when a relationship exists between a person and a spouse's ex, it is generally strained and one or the other, and even both, wish the other person did not exist. The new wife or husband feels the presence of the ex-spouse intruding into the new marriage, often via the stepchildren, even though they may not actually interact with the person. The new husband or wife may feel that the marriage is a triangle rather than a marriage.

> I really don't care for my husband's ex-wife because she will always hold us back. She is always there even though we never see her. Once in a while we have to have the boys visit her or she phones to talk with them. She's got two more but that does not satisfy her. [This remark was made of the only noncustodial mother in the sample who had had a second set of children in her remarriage. It was actually the children's custodial father who prevented them from seeing her.]

> It's not a matter of jealousy but of practicality. When a marriage is over, it is over, period. In my case, it's quite clear and she has no competition because I never saw my former wife but in my wife's case, it's different because they share custody and have to communicate so that we're tied to them in effect. Hopefully, this won't go on forever because the boys are getting older and they're making a lot of their decisions themselves. But I think my wife is over protective. These boys've got to grow up. I am lucky that he's a decent type of person. He does not intrude and he is fair.

The new husband or wife often resents the help the spouse has to give his/her ex, especially financial help.

> I don't really talk with her. She just calls because she wants money and I say just a sec. [...] because she needs too much money. That's the second time I am married to a man who's got to support children and I resent that part because a husband's money ought to be for him and his wife, not his ex-wife. I don't get anything from my previous husband because we didn't have any children. ... She wants him to come over to fix this or that. Really.

> She calls my husband at least once a month. She always needs something. I try to stay out of it because of his children but if it weren't

for the children I'd tell her off. Sometimes we just don't have the money and last winter he gave me a fur coat for Christmas; well, she heard of it and there was no end to it. But I *am* his wife and *I* work each day in the store.

In some instances, the new spouse and the ex-spouse (especially the new wife and the ex-wife) have to cooperate in order to raise each other's children and to arrange visiting schedules so as to not ruin the new wife's life (Ahrons and Wallisch 1987; Petronio 1988).

It's a bit like having an older sister. I even ask her about the baby, how to do things and she doesn't mind. She says I've helped her a lot with her children so it's fine. They [my parents] even think that my stepchildren are quite nice. They find it a bit indecent that I have a good relationship with his ex-wife but they're getting used to it.

She phones me before she comes over and I phone her once to ask her about something. I don't want the boys to go back to her with sweets if she doesn't allow it. I don't want to spoil them too much and they will look back in comparison because I know that children do make these comparisons. So long as I have to keep my stepsons, I might as well get along with their mother.

We have a lot of planning to do to arrange her children's visits. Generally the oldest three drop by a couple of times a month for an afternoon or something like that and his son sleeps over more often than not while the two girls have steadies and go back home. Then her three youngest come for most of the day, Saturday and Sunday, every other weekend. So we have a lot to talk about. But I think she must appreciate me because I don't have to have his children over as often as I do especially so since I have three of my own, so actually I babysit for her. She doesn't [interfere], not exactly, but what can you expect with so many children, it's a real interference even if they're quite good. All in all, we have nine children over at times.

In a few cases, a spouse and a spouse's ex will develop a warm and friendly relationship, although such instances are more rare than certain media stories lead us to believe. Generally, one woman is more in need of assistance than the other.

When she comes for her son she waves at me or she comes in for a minute. Just small talk about this and that and the children. When we drop him off, we may go in. If I am sick or something she'll ask how are you and her husband is very nice too. I am very lucky because ex-wives can be a real problem. She's much older than I am; it's a different generation so there's no competition between us and my husband provides well for his son so she has nothing to complain about. She really minds her business and always asks my husband if it is alright if Doug comes to visit. She always calls before even though Doug calls us too.

Most of the time I just say how are you and wait a second, I'll get Bernie. I know she'd like to talk to me more often. When I have the time I listen to her. She asks for my advice on about everything. She's a good, weak woman. She just has no sense of self, it's incredible. She's lived such a sheltered life. I couldn't be mean to her, she's such a good woman, but terribly immature, she's very friendly and kind.

No, we don't socialize as such but we're friendly and we get along. It would be ridiculous not to. She's a nice person, things just didn't work out with my husband. He got his mid-life crisis early [laughs] and it would be nice if she got remarried but I don't even think she ever dates.

However, even when a friendship is involved, the two persons, ex and current spouse, generally avoid discussing the partner they have shared serially. When asked what they talked about when they met, children and stepchildren were always mentioned first, especially by women. They exchanged information and gossip they believed could be mutually useful: recipes, television programs, films, work were mentioned. Men unavoidably replied: "sports, news, cars," and the like. Conversations between a woman's two "husbands" were less personal than those between a man's two "wives."

A relationship with the spouse's ex seemed facilitated when the new spouse had not been the "cause" of the previous marital breakdown, that is, when the new spouse had not been involved with the other partner in an adulterous relationship.

Which is understandable because when I started my friendship with her husband they had separated temporarily and were supposed to get back together but he never did. She thinks it's because of me while actually my husband tells me it had nothing to do with me;

he was just unhappy in the marriage, he might have gone back but he would not have stayed.

She's always been nice to me because I have never done anything to her. I was not involved in her marital breakup and I didn't have custody of her children, so there is really nothing negative between us; besides she's happily remarried I gather, and as far as I am concerned I am so much younger that I don't feel threatened.

It has been shown that nearly half the respondents never see their spouse's ex and that two-thirds feel that they have no real relationship with that person. Moreover, the likelihood of having a relationship with the spouse's ex is conditional upon the existence of stepchildren and women more than men maintain verbal contacts with that person. Because remarriages are less institutionalized (Cherlin 1978) than marriages, there are no specific ground rules concerning the spouse-ex-spouse relationship. At least, there are no ground rules that are socially sanctioned. But the results of this study imply that there are *implicit* ground rules which in effect dictate that there be no relationship with the spouse's ex unless mandated by the existence of children from the previous marriage. *Another implicit rule is that the spouse serially shared should not be discussed during conversations with the spouse's ex*, and that such conversations remain safely impersonal and focus on the children.

These implicit ground rules become quite explicit when the respondents are asked about them. In fact, respondents were very articulate and opinionated concerning what they should do or not do, should say or not say to the spouse's ex. *Other rules explicitly expressed were to intervene as little as possible in matters concerning the spouse and his/her ex and their shared children*; and when children are involved, it was deemed important to be cordial so as to avoid custody and visiting problems. Therefore, it is on the one hand true that rules governing a relationship with a spouse's ex are not institutionalized if this term is used to mean that they are not encoded in law or etiquette books (although they are starting to be). However, the results clearly indicate that there is a great deal of latent or unspoken consensus, although not necessarily *within* a remarried dyad (see Goetting 1980), concerning certain aspects of this relationship (or potential relationship).

There was also a great deal of uneasiness about the possibility of having a close relationship with that person, in part because of the dangers it could create for the new marriage: new wives and husbands felt that their spouse should be kept away from the ex, except when the welfare of children required his/her presence. When a person did not get along well with his/her ex-spouse, the new spouses often formed a coalition against the ex-spouse. This was perceived as a factor contributing to strengthen the marital unity. Generally, *the former spouse is viewed suspiciously by the new spouse, especially if the former spouse has more of certain socially valued attributes such as youth, beauty, money, success, and children.*

In a monogamous society, the spectre of a marital triangle looms large. In point of fact, serial monogamy does involve a triangle or sets of, and such triangles do not fit well within North American ideology concerning marriage. The new partners often would want to "get rid" of the ex or exes. They would like to have a marriage rather than a remarriage. When there are stepchildren (Messinger, 1976, p. 195), just having a marriage is impossible because the partners are at a starting point which is further ahead on the life span of family life than is the starting point at marriage. Remarriage may involve entire networks of former spouses as will be shown in a later section (Walker and Messinger 1979; Fishman and Hamel 1981), and the spouse's ex becomes a mandatory appendage, albeit generally unwanted, at the very least tolerated. While the new spouses are future oriented, the spouse's ex is a reminder of a past one would rather forget.

RELATIONSHIP WITH EX-SPOUSE'S NEW SPOUSE

The 112 formerly or currently divorced subjects whose first ex-spouse has remarried are the object of this section. This section represents the other side of the coin presented in the previous one where respondents talked about their new spouse's ex; now, this ex-spouse talks about them. Moreover, a great proportion of the respondents overlapped, being at one point the new spouse's ex and at the other point the ex-spouse's new spouse. Therefore, so as not to unduly lengthen the interview sessions, the questions

Table VIII.2. Respondent's Feelings Toward Ex-Spouse's New Spouse

	Respondents' Gender	Respondents' Marital Status Divorced vs. Remarried	Respondents Have Children From Previous Marriage	Where Respondents' Children Live	Respondents' SES	When Ex-spouse Started Dating New Spouse
Respondents' feelings for ex's new spouse	Trend	N.S.	$p < .0016$	N.S.	Trend	$p < .0119$
Ex-spouse's remarriage complicted things for respondents (as perceived by respondents)	Trend	N.S.	$p < .0028$	N.S.	N.S.	$p < .001$

163

asked for the previous section were not, except for one, repeated for the ex-spouse's new spouse.

Respondents were asked about their feelings for their ex-spouse's new spouse, and we tested for differences by the same variables as in Table VIII.1 with two modifications. The key modification consisted in verifying the effect of the time at which the ex-spouse had begun dating the new spouse. We will examine each of the independent variables detailed in Table VIII.2.

More women (32%) than men (21%) liked the ex-spouse's new spouse. Men tended to be more neutral (26% vs. 17%). However, this difference was not statistically significant. Women had more contacts with their ex-spouse's new spouse (which corroborates the results of the previous section) than men in order to mediate visiting arrangements for the children or stepchildren. This necessity to be in contact may explain why women were more positive than men toward the ex-spouse's new spouse.

This explanation is also consistent with the effect of the presence of children from the previous marriage. When there were no children, 64% of the respondents reported not knowing the ex-spouse's new spouse in comparison to 23% of those who had children from the previous marriage. The rest of the respondents with children were equally distributed among the liking, neutral, and disliking categories. Who had custody of the children, however, made no difference.

There was a trend for higher-SES persons to like the ex-spouse's new spouse more often than lower-SES persons (31% vs. 21%) and for lower-SES persons to dislike him/her more often than higher-SES persons (29% vs. 17%). I hypothesize that the ex-spouse's new spouse is a greater threat to lower than higher-SES persons because resources that are scarce have to be partialled out or, at the very least, there is always the threat that they could be. Thus, a deprived lower-SES woman is more likely to resent her ex-husband's new wife than will a higher-SES woman because the lower-SES woman has few resources and considers it unfair if the new spouse has more resources than she. This is well illustrated in a woman's response as to why she resents her ex-husband's new wife: "Because she is a bad influence on my former husband: she encourages him to give me as little as possible."

Another reaction of a different nature:

> At first I resented her because of her two children and because he [her ex-husband] asked that our children visit less often to give her a chance to get used to the situation more slowly.

Many of the negative reactions arose because the new spouse presents a competition for the love of one's children or because he/she presents a psychological or moral threat to the children themselves:

> I told my wife, my ex-wife, that she's got to be very careful never to let the girls alone with him. She was offended but she got the point. I just don't trust him. ... My ex-wife's husband is a burden to me in a way [he is an alcoholic].

> I despise him, not because he married her but because of the children. He's a terrible example, always out of a job, drinking, probably running around, lazy, never home. He has abandoned his own children. There is nothing good he can teach my children and they live in a real slum. We've got to get them out of this before they enter adolescence. I wouldn't mind him had we had no children. I would say she deserves what she gets but it is detrimental to the children's situation.

Because of the children, however, many respondents had begun appreciating their former partner's new spouse or, at the very least, saw the necessity to get along with him or her for the children's sake.

> First, she was always very polite and helpful. Her children were a bit older than mine and she was always kind to my children when they visited. Once in a while she would send them back with deserts she had baked because I worked and she didn't. She knitted for them and would call me to ask their favorite color. She wasn't trying to take over and she always consulted me.

The following woman's ex-husband was in his third marriage. Therefore, because of her children, she has had to cope with her former husband's second ex-wife and his current wife.

We get along very well [ex-husband's second ex-wife]. You could say that we have learned to use each other to get what we need for our children.

It does seem to me that you are getting along as well with your husband's ex-wife as you are with his new wife?

It makes things easier. It helps when you have children that go back and forth. Otherwise it would be a huge headache and I am lucky because they are both level-headed persons.

EX-SPOUSE'S ADULTERY AND REMARRIAGE

Returning to Table VIII.2, it is shown that the only other variable that had a great deal of impact on a person's feelings for his or her ex-spouse's new spouse is the timing of the onset of the relationship. Respondents were asked when their ex-spouse "had met his/her current spouse." The alternatives were:

- while you were still living together;
- during your separation;
- after divorce;
- don't know.

The results from Table VIII.2 are presented in greater detail in Table VIII.3. First, we see that *the most detrimental situation is when the ex-spouse had an extra-marital affair which led to a remarriage to the third party.* This may be a common sense finding but it is not documented in the literature. There were only 12 respondents, or 10.7% of the respondents with a remarried ex-spouse, whose ex-spouse eventually remarried the person they had had an affair with. However, it is possible that a few of the 19 who did not know when the relationship began would fall in this category. (Other adulterous ex-spouses did not marry the third party involved.) Nevertheless the fact remains that most persons who remarry find new spouses *after* they have left their previous spouse.

Only 8.3% of the 12 respondents who believed that the ex-spouse's new spouse had met their ex-spouse during their marriage

Table VIII.3. Respondents' Feelings for Ex-Spouse's New Spouse By Time When Ex-Spouse Started Dating New Spouse

Onset of Dating Between Ex-spouse and Ex's New Spouse	Don't Know Ex-spouse's New Spouse	I Like Ex-spouse's New Spouse	I Feel Neutral	I don't Like/ Resent Ex-spouse's New Spouse	Row Totals
While we were still married	1 8.3* 2.9** .9***	1 8.3 3.2 .9	5 41.7 21.7 4.5	5 41.7 21.7 4.5	12 10.7
During separation	7 18.4 20.0 6.3	16 42.1 51.6 14.3	7 18.3 30.4 6.3	8 21.1 34.8 7.1	38 33.9
After divorce	16 37.2 45.7 14.3	11 25.6 35.5 9.8	9 20.9 39.1 8.0	7 16.3 30.4 6.3	43 38.4
Don't know when they started dating	11 57.9 31.4 9.8	3 15.8 9.7 2.7	2 10.5 8.7 1.8	3 15.8 13.0 2.7	19 17.0
Totals	35 3.13	31 27.7	23 20.5	23 20.5	112 100.0

Notes: * Row percentage. chi-square 21.16580, 9 df., $p < .0119$.
      ** Column percentage.
      *** Total percentage.

liked the new spouse. In terms of promoting liking, initiation of the relationship during the separation was the ideal in this sample. The second best time was after divorce. I surmise that when the ex-spouse begins dating his/her future husband/wife during the separation period (which, in Canada, averaged about three years before the new 1986 legislation), adjustment to this situation occurs before the final, legal arrangements are completed and the child maintenance and visitation aspects are more realistically settled than when the prospect of a remarriage occurs only after legal arrangements have been finalized. The ex-spouse with custody is generally the mother and *she* remarries later than her ex-husband. Therefore, when he meets *his* future wife during separation, he may be more ready to make financial concessions to his ex-wife than if he were not to remarry so soon. Or, still, the ex-wife may feel that she should protect herself and her children and consequently obtains more. Visiting arrangements are generally disturbed by the arrival of a new partner, at least temporarily. If this arrival takes place while the ex-husband still sees his children regularly, during separation, he may be more inclined to arrange his life in such a way that his relationship with his children is not disturbed. In contrast, he may be less inclined to do so several years later when his relationship with his children has waned. His new wife may also be less willing to compromise when a status quo already exists in her favor. During separation, a status quo is not yet in place and the future new wife may be forced by circumstances to cooperate with the ex-wife. The plausibility of these arguments is substantiated by the fact that 37.2% of the respondents whose ex-spouse had met a new partner *after* divorce did not know the person compared to only 18.4% when the new partner had entered the picture *during* the separation period.

Resentment of an adulterous beginning simmers on and remains explosive for many years.

> At first, I hated her. Now I act as if I liked her because we help each other out. In a way, I do like her but I can't forget that she helped break up my marriage.... Most of the time I don't think about it because the past is the past but it still creeps up on me occasionally. I am still very jealous of her and of her children. They look like him and so do mine so our children really belong together, but I resent the fact that hers got to have their cake and eat it too.

Sometimes I wish they'd turn out wrong and go wrong when they are teenagers.

Another woman explains the situation:

> I really felt very bad but both say that they were just friends and became lovers only after my husband left me. Anyway, even if it isn't true, they both have worked very hard at being forgiven. She has often told me she felt very bad about my thinking that she had broken up our marriage. She has worked very hard at keeping the family together. She didn't want me to have with my son the problems she had with hers.

Respondents were also asked how much their ex-spouse's remarriage "had complicated things." The choices were from "very much" to "not at all" and included options indicating that the remarriage had helped. Table VIII.2 illustrates that *women more than men had found that their ex-husband's remarriage had been a problem;* men, however, frequently replied that their ex-wife's remarriage had *helped.* (The difference, however, was not statistically significant.) A follow-up question asked in what ways the remarriage had been a problem and in what ways it had helped. Fifteen men indicated that their ex- wife's remarriage had helped *financially.* These men's ex-wife had custody of their children. Moreover, there was a trend indicating that these men were more often of higher-SES than of lower-SES. In this sample, lower-SES men rarely contributed to their children's maintenance whether or not the children's mother had remarried It is also significant that persons who had responded that their ex-spouse's remarriage had created problems tended to harbor more negative feelings toward the new spouse than other respondents.

It is not surprising that women tended to have been upset by the remarriage more than men: men remarry earlier. Once remarried, these men often "pray" that their ex-wife will also remarry so as to ease their conscience and to lighten their financial load. Moreover, by the time their ex-wife remarries, men are attached to another conjugal unit and detached from the ex-wife. Thus, for these reasons, men are generally less disturbed than women by their ex-spouse's remarriage. They were, however, very upset when she remarried first—especially soon after the divorce, and specially if they themselves had no marital prospects.

Moreover, women have custody of the children: the remarriage is structurally more complicated for them and may also tie down financial resources they need. Table VIII.2 shows that having children from a previous marriage was a very significant variable in raising the perceived level of complications arising from the ex-spouse's remarriage. Further results also indicate that when the ex-spouse began dating his or her future wife or husband during the marriage, or *immediately* upon separating, as opposed to later during the separation, the remarriage is perceived more negatively in terms of consequences for the self. Adultery being one of the grounds for divorce in Canada until 1986, such cases had a relatively brief separation period: divorce followed rapidly and so did remarriage when there was a "built-in" new partner. Similarly, where a serious relationship is initiated *early* on in the separation, the ex-spouses frequently used adultery as a cause in order to obtain a more rapid divorce—generally at the instigation of the remarrying ex-spouse. Thus, the other ex-spouse not only had to suffer the ignominy of having been cheated but had to adjust to the idea that a quick divorce and the ex-spouse's remarriage were upon her.

Such a combination of stressors leads to further problems and it is practically impossible, under such circumstances, to view the ex-spouse's remarriage or the new partner positively. It should be noted here that unless a spouse is herself or himself adulterous or desires to get rid of the other, *adultery was reported by respondents to be a terrible stigma to bear for the offended party*. It brings a sense of defeat, lower self-esteem, and terrible resentment, not to omit moral outrage. An earlier chapter showed that ex-spouses who were still embattled after six years of separation tended to have been adulterous (that is, one of them had been), even though the overall marriage might have been a reasonable one. *Adultery obliterated in one giant sweep all that had been good in the marriage.* The divorce was a tumultuous one as a result; the remarriage and the new spouse were additional battles lost and bred further bitterness.

NETWORKS OF EX-PARTNERS
AND NEW PARTNERS

Chapter III indicated that a continued relationship with an ex-spouse after six years of separation is largely contingent on the presence of shared children. It has also been shown that the same principle applies to relationships between an ex-spouse's new spouse and self, or self with a new spouse's ex-spouse. Moreover, even the presence of children does not guarantee that such relationships will take place. A new type of extended kin system based on these new types of legal relationships was previously discussed. In the domain of divorce and remarriage, the boundaries of the nuclear family become more elastic and include members who no longer live with target respondents as well as new members who are introduced via remarriage (Walker and Messinger 1979). This section explores how often chains of divorced/remarried persons actually become networks or extended kin systems and what are the key factors leading to the establishment of such networks or "linked family systems" (Jacobson 1987).

The literature on network in the area of the sociology of the family has been inspired by the work of Bott (1957, 1971). Following her lead, several studies were mounted in order to address her hypothesis on the relationship between network density and conjugal roles (Aldous and Strauss 1966; Chatterjee 1977; Gordon and Downing 1978; Hannan and Katsiaouni 1977; Kapferer 1973; Noble 1973; Turner 1967; Udry and Hall 1965; Wimberly 1983). Unfortunately, the spurt of studies that followed her inspiration was of short duration, and the field of the family counts few recent inquiries using the network approach (e.g., see Lee 1979; Oliveri and Reiss 1981; Reiss and Oliveri 1983). However, social networks have reappeared in the literature in the area of social support, and network analysis has become important in many other areas, such as in network therapy for an individual or a family (Cohen and Sakolovski 1978), coping, stress (Adams 1974; Belle 1982; Toldsdorf 1976), as well as in the social sciences, even to the point of supporting the creation of a journal *Social Networks*.

This sample has 49 chains that were originated on the basis of the 49 initial respondents from the first wave of interviews (1978-1980). All other respondents in our sample were the ex-spouses and new spouses of these 49 persons, as well as the ex-spouses' new spouses, and the new spouses' ex- spouses.

In order to qualify as a network, a chain had to have a minimum of three adults, and these three persons had to have *at least one interaction* (or relationship) *outside the marital unit,* be it with an ex-spouse or an ex-spouse's new spouse, and so on. Within these requirements, 71% of the 49 chains constituted a network and 28.6% constituted a non-network or a mere chain: the latter were ex-couples or individuals who had nothing to do with each other. Chains averaged only 2.7 persons in comparison to 6.1 for networks.[1]

Second, I wanted to know about the *quality* of the networks: were they mainly positive, mainly negative, or mixed? A positive network is one in which the majority of the interactions are constructive, friendly, and noncombative. (In order to assess quality of network, I used the questions on the quality of the relationships with ex-spouse, ex-spouse's new spouse, and new spouse's ex-spouse.) A negative network is one in which the majority of the interactions are destructive, unfriendly, or quarrelsome. A mixed network contains about half of each of the first two types.

We have seen that 70% of the chains were actual networks. In terms of quality, 40% of the chains were positive networks, 20% were negative networks, and only 10% were mixed (the 30% left were non-networks). Therefore, *only 40% of the chains of divorced/remarried persons constituted positive networks.* However, looking at *networks, we see that over half of them were positive.* Thus, when members of former marriages and their new spouses interact and form a network, they do so in a noncombative and cordial manner more often than otherwise. This finding is somewhat surprising in view of the adversary system of law which exists for divorce, and in view of the fact that, generally, relationships with ex-spouses are not rewarding and affectionate, but are necessitated because of familial, financial, and haphazard reasons. Thus, once necessity requires interaction, the interactants rationally chose to be accommodating rather than combative in order to facilitate their life and that of their children. However, that ex-spouses and their new mates elected to stay away from ex-spouses when they could do so is indicated by the fact that 29% never saw their ex-spouses and never even talked to them on the phone.

Table VIII.4. Quality of Network by Network Density and Average Network Size

	Totals			*Positive*			*Mixed*			*Negative*		
							Quality of Networks					
Density	N	%	X̄ size	N	%	X̄ size	N	%	X̄ size	N	%	X̄ size
High	8	16.3	5.3	5	10.2	5.2	3	6.1	5.3	—	—	—
Medium	15	30.6	5.3	8	16.3	7.6	2	4.1	6.5	5	10.2	4.4
Low	12	24.5	6.3	7	14.3	6.6	—	—	—	5	10.2	6.0
All Networks	35	71.4	6.1	20	40.8	6.7	5	10.2	5.8	10	20.4	5.2
Non Networks	14	28.6	2.7									
All Chains	49	100.0	5.1									

In Table VIII.4, I have divided networks by size, density, and quality. The size of the network simply refers to the number of potential interactants or the number of respondents interviewed in each network. Density refers to the percentage (%) of these potential relationships which are actualized in the network. The formula for determining the density is footnoted.[2] In this study, however, I was interested in relationships *outside* the new marital units or the married couples, as indicated by the interaction lines above the subjects in our diagram.[3]

The following profile emerges. As network size increases, two situations occur. First, the possibility of a non-network decreases because it becomes unlikely that, in a chain of five or more ex-spouses/new spouses, not one interaction would take place on a regular basis. Second, as network size increases, the probability of a high density network decreases: in Table VIII.4, there are no high density networks for networks of 9, 10, and 12 persons. High density networks have an average of 5.3 members as opposed to 6.4 and 6.3 for low and medium density networks. Given that over one fourth of ex-spouses do not interact at all, it would be difficult to find a large network in which all ex-spouses and their new spouses interact. In a metropolitan center which allows for distance, mobility, and anonymity, there is a mathematical and geographic improbability of locating large networks with all members interacting. One could hypothesize that large networks would be much more dense in a village or rural environment with little out-migration and in which anonymity is largely absent because ex-partners and their new mates could not escape from practically "running into each other" on a regular basis (Bott 1957; Cubitt 1973).

A case by case examination of the larger networks shows that they are generally segmented, that is, they are actually constituted of *sub-networks with a high density*, or one such a high density sub-network, while the rest of the members are couples or non-remarried persons who have nothing to do with the others. Therefore, these large networks are acually a theoretical construct rather than a reality from the point of view of the members who neither identify with such a group nor interact with the other members. Rather, the sub-networks are the true networks.

Another finding that emerges from Table VIII.4 is that networks of high density are unlikely to have a negative quality. Thus, high density networks are either positive or mixed in terms of the quality of the interactions. By definition, high density networks have a higher number of interactions, and it has been established (Table not included because of space requirements) that, as the sheer size of a network increases, the possibility of having a "negative" network decreases. Networks of 8 and more respondents have a positive density. Thus, we see that the average size of networks is smallest for negative networks (5.2), intermediate for mixed networks (5.8), and largest for positive networks (6.7). Where members of a large chain go to the trouble of interacting with many others in the chain, they will choose to have pleasant interactions and will avoid the members with whom they would have unpleasant interactions. In contrast, smaller networks do not offer such a structural alternative to their members: they have fewer persons to choose from and persons may *have* to interact with, say, an ex-spouse with whom they do not get along at all.

Finally, if high density networks are either positive or mixed, networks with a low density are either positive or negative—not mixed. This may be because, as low density indicates that few interactions take place, there is less chance of having both negative and positive interactions in a same network. A low density network de facto prevents a wide latitude: it is an "either-or" type of situation.

I also wanted to see how the presence of children from *previous* marriages would be related to network formation, quality, and density. All but two networks contained children from a previous marriage. In contrast, 69% (9 out of 13) of the non-networks or chains had *no* children. Therefore, the mere presence of children contributed to the formation of a network, as anticipated in the results of the previous sections. But there was an apparent contradiction hidden in the data: the four non-networks with children had a much higher average number of children per ex-couple with children (3.3) than networks (2.3).

When using quality of networks as the dependent variable, average number of children showed two differences: (a) high and medium density networks averaged fewer children per ex-couple (2.1 and 2.2 respectively) than low density networks which had 2.8 children on the average per ex-couple. This difference follows the pattern of the previous finding in that a large number of children seemed to be related to a lower density or, in other words, less interaction among the ex-partners and among their new spouses. Similarly (b), positive and mixed networks tended to average slightly fewer children than negative networks, 2.1, 2.0, and 2.4 respectively.

Networks in which the average number of children was smaller seemed to be more positive and especially more cohesive. Also, divorces involving a higher average of children tended to be found in non-networks. These results seem to indicate that broken families had more difficulties maintaining contact when there were more children, *perhaps because the opportunities for conflict increase with a larger number of children* as more decisions have to be made, more money has to be spent, more child-related difficulties may present themselves, and the visitation arrangements become more complex and can, as a consequence, lead to no visitation as a form of conflict resolution. In terms of exchange theory, such situations provide few benefits that could convince the adults to interact. Thus, no exchange takes place in order to satisfy individuals' need for rewards and avoidance of negative events (Thibaut and Kelly 1959).

In addition, the possibility that other variables, such as socioeconomic status, may be involved in this relationship between number of children and network density has to be considered. SES was the key variable chosen simply because previous analyses from this study (published and unpublished) pointed to this variable, along with gender as a key in understanding divorce. Moreover, Udry and Hall (1965) have posited that Bott's analysis may be more relevant to working-class networks than others, indicating SES as a major determinant of network structure. Burt's (1983) findings also point to SES variables as important elements of network analysis.

In view of this, my next line of inquiry was to see if there existed differences in SES between networks and non-networks, and between networks of varying quality. In order to achieve this, I averaged the SES scores of all the members of each chain (network and non-network). Each chain received an average SES score. Although this method can be open to criticism, it is the only one available. It is a good method for homogeneous networks, that is, networks in which the members tend to be all low or high on the SES. But it is a less adequate method when some members are high, others average, and still others low. I looked at SES from the point

Table VIII.5. Network Members' Average Income*
By Quality of Network and Network Density

Network Density	Positive	Quality of Network Mixed	Negative	Total Income Averages
High	5.6	3.9	—	*5.0*
Medium	4.4	5.2	5.3	*4.8*
Low	4.3	—	4.2	*4.3*
Non-Networks 3.7				
Total Income Averages	4.7	4.4	4.7	*4.3*

Note: * Scale from 0 to 8 where 0 = income less than $5,000/year.

of view of education, income, and occupational prestige separately. For space considerations, only the table pertaining to income is presented (see Table VIII.5).

On all three indicators of SES, low density networks had the lowest overall average when compared to high and medium density networks. Thus, networks which had relatively fewer interactions among ex-spouses and their mates tended to be populated by persons who scored lower on the socioeconomic scales. However, non-networks scored even lower by a wide margin than low density networks. Therefore, there was a greater likelihood that ex-spouses and their spouses would interact when they were better educated and had a higher income. On the axis of quality there was no consistent relationship between the SES indicators and network quality.

This inquiry began by asking if SES might contribute to explain the observed relationship between low network density and high average number of children. Indeed, the four non-networks with a higher average of children were of lower SES, as were generally low density networks with a higher average of children. *The combination of a low SES and a higher average of children contributed to prevent ex-spouses from interacting;* in such situations the custodial parents truly headed monoparental families until remarriage.

Presence of children from previous marriages differentiated networks from non-networks but, also, a higher average number of children and a low SES contributed to the creation of a low density network or a non-network rather than a network. Although the size of a chain was the decisive factor in the probability that the chain would become a network or a non-network, when this variable was controlled for, the presence of children became the pivotal variable, and the number of children may even influence the magnitude of the density as well as the quality of the interactions involved.

When children exist from a previous marriage, this previous marriage, however, generally has other traits that in themselves may contribute to a continuation of interaction with an ex-spouse. For instance, such unions were more likely to involve the economic dependency of a mother vis-à-vis the father while childless unions were less likely to foster such a dependency. Second, when there were good economic conditions in the family, the subsequent division of property may have created post-separation ties, including the financial support of the children. In contrast to this, the non-networks and low-density networks included most cases of paternal desertion in the sample and these fathers were of lower SES. Cases of paternal desertion at higher-SES levels were rare.

We have seen that the size of a chain is the first variable which contributed to explain the magnitude and quality of the network density (and the existence of non-networks). Second comes presence or absence of children, as well as average number of children. But SES was of great importance in determining the magnitude of network density, with a higher average SES being more conducive to high network density. This finding is interesting from still another perspective: studies of kinship interaction have found that lower-SES persons were more involved in closer-knit kin systems than middle-class persons (Adams 1968; Hendrix 1976, p. 100). However, these studies have yet to focus on ex-affinal relationships or ex-marital relationships as a form of kin system. Ex-affinal and ex-spousal relationships are not based on the same motives. Therefore, ex-marital networks have rules of interaction which may be distinctive and would be important to study. Quasi-kin or extended family systems were more likely to occur with the presence of a "reasonable" rather than large number of children as well as under secure financial conditions. Poverty and large families seem to impede the formation of these new types of extended family systems which, when positive, can be so functional to the individuals involved. *Poorer divorced/remarried families were more isolated from their kin and quasi-members, as well as from the rest of society.*

NOTES

1. The following questions constituted the indicators of networks: How often did respondents see their ex-spouse, their ex-spouse's new spouse, and their new spouse's ex-spouse? How often did they talk to these persons over the phone? It was decided that the respondents had to see/talk to a person at least three or four times a year in order for a relationship to exist. If respondents indicated that no relationship existed, it was recorded as such.

2. Density $= \dfrac{100 \times Na}{\frac{1}{2} N (N-1)}$ or $\dfrac{\text{Percentage of actual relations}}{\text{theoretically possible relations}}$

where Na refers to the number of actualized relationships and N refers to the number of persons in the network (an application from Barnes as quoted in Niemeijer [1973]).

3. The formula was revised as follows:

$$D = \frac{100 \times \text{non-marital } Na}{[\frac{1}{2} N (N-1)] - \text{Marital units}}$$

where non-marital Na refers to the number of actualized relationships that do not involve a husband or wife currently married to each other. Marital units refers to the number of married couples.

Chapter IX

Conclusions

My previous marriage is merely a footnote in my life.
—Woman, career

Being divorced is not so hard in itself, it's being poor which is.
—Woman, custodial mother on welfare

My divorce was a pathetic waste, a waste of time and a psychological waste. We could have stayed together; instead we chose to subject each other to all manners of psychological warfare.
—Man, executive

Divorce is a real comedy after which comes a second one: remarriage.
—Man, teacher

Divorce is when I started growing up.
—Woman, graduate student

I have wasted four years divorcing and getting over it. Am I better off? I could only answer this question in ten years because this is how long I had been married then.
—Man, professional

This chapter is not meant to be all-encompassing: the previous chapters contain thorough discussion and conclusion sections. Rather, I have chosen to amplify some points and to draw out the breadth of the research that still needs to be carried out. I have also opted to emphasize certain gaps which exist in the literature in certain areas of concern to this book.

In Chapter II, I recounted not only the difficulties inherent to locating a large number of custodial fathers and noncustodial mothers, but also showed that custodial fathers who *seek* custody of their children earn on the average a higher income than other divorced fathers. The implications of these results are that paternal custody which is voluntary is likely to remain the preserve of the more affluent fathers. Such fathers have the means to impress a judge, to hire a lawyer, and to pay for a housekeeper or other suitable home arrangement. Other results also indicated that such fathers also had the means to remarry younger, childless women who would help them in their task. They also have more male than female children, and children who are beyond the infant and pre-school stage. Custodial fathers by choice seem to avoid infants and preschoolers: I surmise that the emotional and career costs of the intensive care required by very young children is too high for most men in this society.

While Mendes's study (1976) divided custodial fathers between "seekers" and "assenters," it is interesting that it is not deemed relevant to so categorize custodial mothers. That all women wish to keep their children is probably taken for granted. Yet, in the course of the interviews, it became obvious that many mothers were "assenters" and would have preferred shared custody or paternal custody—especially mothers with difficult children (Rosenblum 1986). In fact, many mothers were even less than assenters: they were "reluctant," but they had had no other socially acceptable alternative.

This result would deserve further study. It is true that most mothers, given the choice, would still seek custody. Nevertheless, during conversations with some mothers, it was obvious that they would *not dare admit* that they would prefer *not* to have their children—even if they had the choice. Therefore, obtaining the confidence of women during a study is essential if sensitive and socially unacceptable feelings are to be divulged. The perceived social stigma is too great for these women: they prefer to have custody so as to be adjudged "normal" mothers or "good" mothers. Similarly, although this topic has not been discussed in this book, noncustodial mothers were judged more harshly by society. They reported having "to do a lot more explaining" than a noncustodial father has to do.

The matter of custody in our society suffers from the double standard in more than one way. Noncustodial mothers, especially of younger children, are stigmatized; custodial fathers can only be so under certain preferable circumstances; custodial mothers are treated as if they all wanted to care and could care for their children. Although this result was serendipitous, it nevertheless indicated how *maternal situations and feelings varied from mother to mother* and how far more this was so than expected.

In the same vein, it may not be all that surprising that the stepmothering experience was found to be a far more complex one than stepfathering. It was shown that live-in stepchildren were a more advantageous situation for women's marital lives than having stepchildren who live with their own mother. The former situation, although a more complex one, was also one that gave greater control to the new couple and more personal satisfaction. But few stepmothers have live-in stepchildren. Most stepmothers play an outsider role when their stepchildren visit and accrue more housework in the bargain. The situation, therefore, leads to a great deal of frustration and stress. The stepmother role is not helped either by the fact that only one third of children see their noncustodial father on a regular basis. The children's resentment, not to mention their own mother's, reflects poorly on the father's new wife.

There has been a recent wave of "positive" books on the topics of remarriage and stepparenting. A rosy picture is occasionally presented and advice on how to reach this blessed state is given. I suspect that this new trend is a reaction to past negativism about reconstituted families and is, consequently, a means to revalue this demographically unavoidable situation. Nevertheless, one should not lose perspective of the fact that reconstituted families, as they are called, involve rewards as well as a great deal of costs. The costs fall more heavily on children as at least one study has found that stepchildren leave the nest earlier than children with their own parents (White and Booth 1985). Either parents are in a hurry to be on their own or these children are. White et al. (1985) found stepchildren to become more attached to their stepfather (even to the detriment of the noncustodial father) when the stepfather does not bring in stepsiblings and when a new child is born to the marriage. Children trade one family for another. One can only wonder, with White et al., at what costs, although this question is asked strictly within the context of a society which places a heavy role on the effect of parents on child development.

There are two currents in the literature that may be conflicting: books giving a flair of normalcy to this trading of one parent for another, juxtaposed with other research in child development and juvenile delinquency placing a heavy emphasis on a continued relationship and identification with two parents. Studies on stepchildren who basically lose contact with the noncustodial parent may indicate that *parents may be less necessary than hitherto believed and are less pivotal in child development than indicated in textbooks.* The study of stepparenting may force further study of parenting or the importance of it. Or still, we may not yet have discovered the negative long-term impact of trading one parent for a stepparent or for no second parent at all. Whatever slant is used, the topic begs for answers and for the right questions to be asked.

The relationship between ex-spouses is a very thorny issue for most divorced and even remarried persons. Few maintain a good relationship with their ex-spouse and those who do tend to be parents. The necessity to coparent or even to see one's children after separation generally requires a reasonably good relationship with one's ex-spouse; however, parents generally have difficulties in their ex-spousal relationship. Actually, the situation should be rephrased as: ex-spouses often have difficulties relating to each other *because* they share children. These children *force* the ex-spouses to relate to each other when they would prefer to forget about each other. In fact, children (and money) are the main elements of contention between ex-spouses while being at the same time the link between them. Very few are the ex-couples who do not use their children against each other at least a few times during separation and even divorce. The structure of the divorce situation in our society is such that few ex-spouses do not sin in this direction. The temptation may be too great as few other alternatives (retaliatory and conciliatory) exist.

The ideal situation for divorce is where the ex-spouses are young, childless, and financially independent of each other. *These adjectives are even more important to a successful divorce for women than for men.* Indeed, women who divorce after 35 have a much lower chance of remarrying and of remarrying a man in their age cohort. The *option* to remarry is important, even when one *chooses not* to remarry. Not having the option because of masculine preference for younger women is cruel. Choosing not to remarry after one has had that option then becomes a lifestyle choice rather than a cruel imposition.

Childless divorces were generally happier than divorces involving children: the ex-spouses did not need to maintain a relationship and the women were less likely to be dependent upon their ex-husband (or welfare). While divorce is generally an emotional catastrophe for children at least temporarily, children are an added stressor for their parents in a majority of the divorce cases. At the same time, I have found in other analyses of my data that, for certain types of parents, children are an important emotional asset and even personal stabilizer in cases of separation/ divorce. This was particularly so for custodial fathers (as most are "seekers") and for custodial mothers who were financially secure and were able to provide adequately for themselves and their children. In statistical analyses not presented in this book, I have found that the custodial fathers and the custodial mothers who had a career utilized fewer medical drugs than the other divorced persons in the sample (with the exception of young, childless divorced), had a lower rate of treatment for emotional problems, felt happier, and had a greater sense of control over their life (Ambert 1982b, 1989).

The ex-spousal relationship, is not a necessity when one can fly alone (childless and financially/socially independent): for such respondents, it is not even a topic worth studying. On the other side of the spectrum are those few ex-spouses who share children and get along very well. The relationship is mutually supportive, even when both are remarried. Children of such divorces probably have the feeling of truly belonging to a two-household family in comparison to other children whose parents rarely see each other or, when they do, continue their quarrels. I have reported that such ex-spouses generally had had a non-stormy end to their marriage and this had prevented post-separation animosity. Such ex-spouses were also more likely to be successful at obtaining their new spouse's cooperation in forming an extended quasi-kin system to everyone's benefit.

However, while there is praise of the benefits of an extended quasi-kin system, it should be pointed out that such a system can be detrimental to the new spouses when it is forced on them. Indeed, most new spouses of divorced persons want to remarry but have never had plans to become stepparents or to become part of a two-household family with an ex-spouse lurking in the shadows. The personalities introduced are important in the adjustment process. Equally important may be the preexisting life situation.

It is said that remarriages may have a higher failure rate than first marriages. However, Aguirre and Paar (1982) found that a husband's previous marital status is a better predictor of a woman's marital stability than her own marital status is. Women who married divorced men were more likely to divorce. Chapter VI questioned whether or not this was due to the large age gap that often exists in such unions; that is, when a divorced man remarries a much younger woman, especially when she had been previously single. Such unions included many unhappy women. Unfortunately, my sample did not include a sufficient number of young divorced women who had remarried single men to draw an adequate comparison. Is it better to remarry another divorced person? Is it preferable for a woman to do so? Or for a man? I doubt that there is a magical, ideal combination of previous marital statuses in a remarriage. The partners' ages, relative ages, and parental status are of such fundamental importance that these variables may be more determining than one's previous marital status or the particular combination of previous marital statuses.

In view of the well-known fact that remarriages involve larger age differences than first marriages, it is somewhat surprising that sociologists have not studied the ramifications of having two persons belonging to different life stages marry. This is the more surprising since there is a burgeoning literature in adult development with a focus on different life stages and how people adjust to ageing. All the indications point to potential difficulties where, for instance, a middle-aged man who is thinking of his future retirement marries a 28 year-old woman who is beginning a career and wants children—or may want children in a few years. Earlier studies have pointed out that sociologists have a high divorce rate. Male university professors often remarry graduate students or other women who are younger than they. It is possible that their own age differences may be an unconscious threat which bars them from studying the topic. It is also possible that an age difference is irrelevant among academics, and that shared intellectual interests are the determining variable.

Whatever the case is, what may be good for academics may not apply for the rest of the population. The research results herein discussed clearly showed potential problems stemming from a large age gap between new spouses. If the topic is carried one step further into the area of stepparenting, it would also be interesting to know how this age difference relates to being a happy or unhappy stepparent. Do younger stepparents of teenagers do better than middle-age stepparents? How do stepchildren relate to a younger versus an older stepparent?

The previous discussion is merely a sample of conclusions drawn from the results and of questions asked from these results. They were also topics that had a salience of their own during the analysis of the results (including many results not presented in this book but discussed in other reports). As this study indicates, there is a great deal more that needs to be known about ex-spouses and new spouses and the many relationships which result. Some topics are even less researched than others and this prevents a well-balanced overview of the field of enquiry. Especially important are longitudinal studies, including studies of persons after they remarry and studies of children of divorce after they become adult (provided they had been studied during the divorce as well).

Long-term studies are one necessity. The second is the in-depth study, that is, the one which allows respondents to speak for themselves, to qualify their answers, and to explain their feelings. Studies are needed in which the main researchers have carried out at least some of the interviews themselves so as to situate their analysis within a real and human context. Statistics alone can mean very little, however complex they are. I suggest that being face-to-face with a respondent for three hours and absorbing the *entire* context of this person's life *explains* far more than statistics in terms of *processes.*

Studies are needed in which both ex-spouses in a divorce and both spouses in a remarriage are interviewed. It is often said that there are two sides to a story. But, as shown in this book, this is not always true: some ex-spouses hold a very similar view on their past marriage and their current relationship with each other. Many, however, hold different views and have undergone *radically different experiences* within a same couple. For the latter, it is not a matter of "two sides to any story" but of two separate life situations. Often, it was a "his and a hers" experience, in Jessie Bernard's words, but, at other points, the experience was genderless. The deeply unhappy spouse could as well be a man as a woman. Therefore, the couple perspective offers a more complete grasp of a divorce and remarriage than do studies of men and women unrelated to each other.

Social class is another aspect of divorce and remarriage which is practically neglected in studies. Yet, this book and other reports show how different the marital and post-marital life conditions of lower-SES men and women were compared to those of more privileged persons. Although I was not able to include class in all the analyses so as to retain some form of coherence, when I did, the results were striking: remarriages at the lower-end of the SES spectrum are much less likely to be happy, and so are divorces. The data clearly indicated that, in terms of marital life, *lower-SES women* were the least fulfilled categories of persons. I suggest that large-sample studies should inquire into the quality of the stepparenting experience by social class. There is not one single published study that has done so. Yet, all information available in the sociological literature point to social class as a key variable over the entire spectrum of life experiences. This should include stepparenting, divorce, remarriage, as well as relationships between ex-spouses and network among them.

Bibliography

Adams, B.N. 1968. *Kinship in an Urban Setting*. Chicago: Markhane.

―――――. 1974. "The Kin Network and the Adjustment of the Ungandan Asians." *Journal of Marriage and the Family* 36: 190-195.

Adams, O. 1988. "Divorce Rates in Canada." *Canadian Social Trends* 11: 18-19.

Aguirre, B.E., and W.C. Parr. 1982. "Husbands' Marriage Order and the Stability of First and Second Marriages of White and Black Women." *Journal of Marriage and the Family* 44: 605-620.

Ahrons, C.R. 1979. "The Binuclear Family: Two Households, One Family." *Alternative Lifestyles* 2: 499-441.

―――――. 1980. "Redefining the Divorced Family: A Conceptual Framework." *Social Work* 6: 437-441.

Ahrons, C.R., and M.E. Bowman. 1981. "Analysis of Couple Data: Theoretical and Methological Issues." Working Paper. Milwaukee, WI: Pre-Conference Workshop on Theory Construction and Research Methodology.

Ahrons, C.R., and L. Wallisch. 1986. "The Relationship Between Former Spouses." In *Close Relationships: Development, Dynamics and Deterioration,* edited by S. Duck and D. Pearlman. Beverly Hills: Sage.

189

————. 1987. "Parenting in the Bi-nuclear Family: Relationships Between Biological and Stepparents." In *Remarriage and Stepparenting: Current Research and Theory*, edited by K. Pasley and M. Ihinger-Tallman. New York: Guilford Press.

Ahrons, C.R., and R.H. Rodgers. 1987. *Divorced Families*. New York: W.W. Norton.

Albrecht, S.L. 1980. "Reactions and Adjustment to Divorce: Difference in the Experiences of Males and Females." *Family Relations* 29: 59-68.

Aldous, J., and M.A. Strauss. 1966. "Social Networks and Conjugal Roles: A Test of Bott's Hypothesis." *Social Forces* 44: 576-580.

Ambert, A.-M. 1982a. "Differences in Children's Behavior Toward Custodial Mothers and Custodial Fathers." *Journal of Marriage and the Family* 44: 73-86.

————. 1982b. "Drug Use in Separated/Divorced Persons: Gender, Parental Status, and Socioeconomic Status." *Social Science and Medicare* 16: 971-976.

————. 1983. "Separated Women and Remarriage Behavior: A Comparison of Financially Secure Women and Financially Insecure Women." *Journal of Divorce* 6: 43-54.

————. 1984. "Longitudal Changes in Children's Behavior Toward Custodial Parents." *Journal of Marriage and the Family* 46: 463-467.

————. 1985. "The Effect of Divorce on Women's Attitude Toward Feminism." *Sociological Focus* 18: 265-272.

————. 1988. "Relationship with Former In-Laws After Divorce: A Research Note." *Journal of Marriage and the Family* 50: 679-686.

————. forthcoming. "Trajectory of Treatment for Emotional Problems Among Divorced/Remarried Persons: An Explanatory Study."

Arendell, T. 1986. *Mothers and Divorce*. Berkeley: University of California Press.

Arnold, R. 1980. "Separation and After." Mimeograph. Toronto: Ontario Ministry of Community and Social Services.

Atkinson, M.P., and B.L. Glass. 1985. "Marital Age Heterogamy and Homogamy, 1900 to 1980." *Journal of Marriage and the Family* 47: 685-691.

Ball, D., P.C. McKenry, and S. Price-Bonham. 1983. "Use of Repeated-measure Designs in Family Research." *Journal of Marriage and the Family* 45: 385-896.

Belle, D. 1982. "Who Uses Mental Health Facilities?" In *The Mental Health of Women,* edited by Guttentag et al. New York: Academic Press.

Bernard, J. 1956. *Remarriage: A Study of Marriage.* Hinsdale, IL: Dryden Press.

_____. 1973. *The Future of Marriage.* New York: Macmillian.

Blau, P.M. 1964. *Exchange and Power in Social Life.* New York: Wiley.

Blishen, B., and H.A. Roberts. 1976. "A Revised Socioeconomic Index for Occupations in Canada." *Canadian Review of Sociology and Anthropology* 13: 71-79.

Blood, R. and M. Blood. 1978. *Marriage.* New York: The Free Press.

Bloom, B., and K.R. Kindle. 1985. "Demographic Factors In the Continuing Relationship Between Former Spouses." *Family Relations* 34: 375-381.

Bohannan, P. 1975. *Stepfathers and the Mental Health of Their Children.* La Jolla, CA: La Jolla Western Behavioral Service Institute.

_____. 1971. "Divorce Chains, Households of Remarriage, and Multiple Divorces." In *Divorce and After,* edited by P. Bohannan. Garden City, NY: Anchor Books.

Bokemeier, J., and P. Monroe. 1983. "Continued Reliance on One Respondent in Family Decision-making Studies: A Content Analysis." *Journal of Marriage and the Family* 45: 645-652.

Booth, A., and S. Welch. 1978. "Spousal Consensus and Its Correlates." *Journal of Marriage and the Family* 40: 23-32.

Bott, E. 1957. *Family and Social Network.* New York: Free Press.

Boulton, M.G. 1983. *On Being a Mother.* London: Tavistock.

Bowerman, C.E., and D.P. Irish. 1962. "Some Relationships of Stepchildren to Their Parents." *Marriage and Family Living* 24: 113-121.

Brody, G.H., E. Neubaum, and R. Forehand. 1988. "Serial Marriage: A Heuristic Analysis of an Emerging Family Form." *Psychological Bulletin* 103: 211-222.

Brown, D. 1982. *The Stepfamily: A Growing Challenge for Social Work.* Social Work Monographs. University of East Anglica.

Brown, P., B.J. Felton, V. Whiteman, and R. Manela. 1980. "Attachment and Distress Following Marital Separation." *Journal of Divorce* 3: 303-317.

Bumpass, L.L., and J.A. Sweet. 1972. "Differentials in Marital Instability: 1970." *American Sociological Review* 37: 754-766.

Burgoyne, J., and D. Clark. 1982a. "Reconstituted Families: In *Families in Britian,* edited by R.N. Rapoport, M.F. Fogarty and R. Rapoport. London: Routledge & Kegan Paul.

―――――. 1982b. "From Father to Stepfather." In *The Father Figure,* edited by L. McGee and M. O'Brien. London: Tavistock.

―――――. 1984. *Making A-Go-Of-It. A Study of Stepfamilies in Sheffield.* London: Routledge & Kegan Paul.

Burt, R.S. 1978. "Applied Network Analysis; An Overview." *Sociological Methods and Research* 7: 123-130.

―――――. 1983. "Distinguishing Contents." In *Applied Network Analysis,* edited by R.S. Burt and M.J. Minor. Beverly Hills: Sage.

Byrd, A.J., and R.M. Smith. 1988. "A Qualitative Analysis of the Decision to Remarry Using Gilligan's Ethic of Care." *Journal of Divorce* 11: 87-102.

Bytheway, W.R. 1981. "The Variation with Age of Age Differences in Marriage." *Journal of Marriage and the Family* 43: 923-927.

Carter, H., and P.C. Glick. 1976. *Marriage and Divorce: A Social and Economic Study.* Rev. ed. Cambridge: Harvard University Press.

Chatterjee, M. 1977. "Conjugal Roles and Social Network in an Indian Urban Sweeper Locality." *Journal of Marriage and the Family* 39: 193-202.

Cherlin, A. 1977. "The Effect of Children on Marital Dissolution." *Demography* 14: 265-272.

―――――. 1978. "Remarriage as an Incomplete Institution." *American Journal of Sociology* 84: 634-649.

―――――. 1981. *Marriage, Divorce, Remarriage.* Cambridge: Harvard University Press.

Clingempeel, W.G. 1981. "Quasi-kin Relationships and Marital Quality in Stepfather Families." *Journal of Personality and Social Psychology* 5: 890-901.

Clingempeel, W.G., E. Brand, and S. Segal. 1987. "A Multilevel Multivariable-developmental Perspective for Future Research on Stepfamilies." In *Remarriage and Stepparenting,* edited by K. Pasley and M. Ihinger-Tallman. New York: Guilford Press.

Clingempeel, W.G., R. Ievoli, and E. Brand. 1984. "Structural Complexity and the Quality of Stepfather Stepchild Relationship." *Family Process* 23: 547-560.

Cohen, C.I. and J. Sakolovsky. 1978. "Schizophrenia and Social Networks." *Schizophrenia Bulletin* 4: 546-560.

Cornell, L.L. 1989. "Gender Differences in Remarriage After Divorce in Japan and the United States." *Journal of Marriage and the Family* 51: 457-464.

Counts, R.M., and K. Reid. 1987. "A Comparison of Men Who are Divorce Prone With Those Who are Marriage Phobic." *Journal of Divorce* 10: 69-86.

Cubitt, T. 1973. "Network Density Among Urban Families." In *Network Analysis,* edited by J. Boissevain and J.C. Mitchell. The Hague: Mouton.

Day, R., and W. MacKey. 1981. "Redivorce Following Remarriage: A Reevaluation." *Journal of Divorce* 4: 39-47.

Dean, G., and D.T. Gurak, 1978. "Marital Homogamy the Second Time Around." *Journal of Marriage and the Family* 40: 559-570.

Defrain, J., and B. Eirick. 1987. "Coping as Divorced Single Parents: A Comparative Study of Fathers and Mothers." *Family Relations* 30: 265-274.

Duberman, L. 1973. "Step-kin Relationships." *Journal of Marriage and the Family* 35: 283-292.

————. 1975. *The Reconstituted Family.* New York: Nelson Hall.

Eekelaar, J., and E. Clive. 1977. *Custody After Divorce.* Oxford: Centre for Sociolegal Studies, Social Science Research Council.

Fast, I., and A.C. Cain. 1966. "The Stepparent Role: Potential for Disturbances in Family Functioning." *American Journal of Orthopsychiatry* 36: 485-491.

Ferri, E. 1976. *Growing up in a One-Parent Family: A Long-Term Study of Child Development.* London: NFER Publishing Co.

_____. 1984. *Stepchildren in the National Child Development Study*. London: National Children's Bureau.

Fishman, B., and B. Hamel. 1981. "From Nuclear to Stepfamily Idealogy: A Stressful Change." *Alternative Lifestyles* 2: 181-204.

Fox, E. 1983. *The Marriage-Go-Round*. New York: University Press of America.

Furstenberg, F.F., Jr. 1982. "Conjugal Succession: Reentering Marriage After Divorce." In *Life-Span Development and Behavior*, vol. 4., edited by B. Baltes and O. Brim, Jr. New York: Academic Press.

_____. 1987a. "Marital Description and Child Care." In *Child Support in International Perspective*, edited by S.B. Kamerman and A.J. Kahn. Beverly Hills: Sage.

_____. 1987b. "The New Extended Family: The Experience of Parents and Children After Remarriage." In *Remarriage and Stepparenting*, edited by K. Pasley and M. Ihinger-Tallman. New York: Guilford Press.

Furstenberg, F.F., Jr., and C.W. Nord. 1985. "Parenting Apart: Patterns of Childrearing After Marital Disruption." *Journal of Marriage and the Family* 47: 893-904.

Furstenberg, F.F., Jr., and G.B. Spanier. 1984. *Recycling the Family, Remarriage after Divorce*. Beverly Hills: Sage.

Gangon, L.H., and M. Coleman. 1988. "Do Mutual Children Cement Bonds in Stepfamilies?" *Journal of Marriage and the Family* 50: 687-698.

Glenn, N.D., and K. Kramer. 1987. "The Marriages and Divorces of the Children of Divorce." *Journal of Marriage and the Family* 49: 813-825.

Glenn, N.D., and C.N. Weaver. 1977. "The Marital Happiness of Remarried Divorced Persons." *Journal of Marriage and the Family* 39: 331-337.

Glick, P.C. 1980. "Remarriage: Some Recent Changes and Variations." *Journal of Family Issues* 1: 455-479.

_____. 1984. "Marriage, Divorce, and Living Arrangements: Prospective Changes." *Journal of Family Issues* 5: 7-26.

_____. 1989. "Remarried Families, Stepfamilies, and Stepchildren: A Brief Demographic Profile." *Family Relations* 38: 24-27.

Glick, P.C. and A.J. Norton. 1977. "Marrying, Divorcing, and Living Together in the U.S. Today." *Population Bulletin* 32: 5.

Goetting, A. 1980. "Former Spouse-Current Spouse Relationships." *Journal of Family Issues* 1: 58-80.

————. 1981. "Divorce Outcome Research: Issues and Perspectives." *Journal of Family Issues* 2: 350-378.

Goldsmith, J. 1980. "Relationship Between Former Spouses: Descriptive Findings." *Journal of Divorce* 4: 120.

Goode, W.J. 1956. *Women in Divorce.* New York: Free Press.

Gordon, M., and H. Downing. 1978. "A Multivariate Test of the Bott Hypothesis in an Urban Irish Setting." *Journal of Marriage and the Family* 40: 585-593.

Gove, W.R., and M.R. Geerken. 1977. "The Effect of Children and Employment on the Mental Health of Married Men and Women." *Social Forces* 56: 66-76.

Grief, G. 1985. *Single Fathers.* Lexington, MA: Lexington Books.

Griffith, J.D., H.P. Koo, and C.M. Suchindram. 1985. "Childbearing and Family in Remarriage." *Demography* 22: 73-88.

Guisinger, S., P.A. Cowan, and D. Schuldberg. 1989. "Changing Parent and Spouse Relations in the First Year of Remarriage of Divorced Fathers." *Journal of Marriage and the Family* 51: 445-456.

Gurak, D.T., and G. Dean. 1979. "The Remarriage Market: Factors Influencing the Selection of Second Husbands." *Journal of Divorce* 3: 161-173.

Hannan, D.F., and L.A. Katsiaouni. 1977. *Traditional Families? From Culturally Prescribed to Negotiated Roles in Farm Families.* Dublin: Economic and Social Research Institute.

Harper, P. 1984. "Children in Stepfamilies; Their Legal and Family Status." Policy Background Paper No. 4. Melbourne: Institute of Family Studies.

Hendrix, L. 1976. "Kinship, Social Networks, and Integration Among Ozark Residents and Out-Migrants." *Journal of Marriage and the Family* 38: 97-104.

Hetherington, E.M. 1987. "Family Relations Six Years After Divorce." In *Remarriage and Stepparenting*, edited by K. Pasley and M. Ihinger-Tallman. New York: Guilford Press.

Hetherington, E.M., M. Cox, and R. Cox. 1978. "The Aftermath of Divorce." In *Mother/Child, Father/Child Relationships.*

edited by J.H. Stevens, Jr. and M. Mathews. The National Association for the Education of Young Children.

————. 1979. "Stress and Coping in Divorce: A Focus on Women." Pp. 95-128 in *Psychology and Women: In Transition,* edited by Jeanne E. Gullahorn. Washington, DC: Winston & Sons.

————. 1982. "Effects of Divorce on Parents and Children." In *Nontraditional Families: Parenting and Child Development.* edited by M.E. Lamb. Hillsdale, NJ: Lawrence Erlbaum.

Hewlett, S.A. 1986. *A Lesser Life. The Myth of Women's Liberation in America.* New York: William Morrow.

Hobart, C. 1988. "The Family System in Remarriage: An Exploratory Study." *Journal of Marriage and the Family* 50: 649-661.

Hoffman, S. and J. Holmes. 1976. "Husbands, Wives, and Divorce. Pp. 23-76 in *Five Thousand American Families* vol. 4, edited by G. J. Duncan and J. N. Morgan. Ann Arbor, MI: The University of Michigan Survey Research Center.

Homans, G.C. 1961. *Social Behavior.* New York: Harcourt, Brace and World.

Houseknecht, S.K. 1979. "Childless and Marital Adjustment." *Journal of Marriage and the Family* 41: 259-266.

Jackson, B. 1982. "Single-parent Families." In *Families in Britain.* edited by R.N. Rapoport, M.P. Fogarty, and R. Rapoport. London: Routledge & Kegan Paul.

Jacobson, D.S. 1979. "Stepfamilies: Myths and Realities." *Social Work* 24: 202-207.

————. 1987. "Family Type, Visiting Patterns, and Children's Behavior in the Stepfamily: A Linked Family System." In *Remarriage and Stepparenting,* edited by K. Pasley and M. Ihinger-Tallman. New York: Guilford Press.

Jorgensen, S.R., and D.M. Klein. 1979. "Sociocultural Heterogamy, Dissension, and Conflict in Marriage." *Pacific Sociological Review* 22: 51-75.

Kalbach, W.W., and W.W. McVey, Jr. 1976. "The Canadian Family: A Demographic Profile." Pp. 94-108 in *The Canadian Family in Comparative Perspective,* edited by L.E. Larson. Scarborough: Prentice-Hall.

Kapferer, B. 1973. "Social Network and Conjugal Roles in Urban Zambia: Towards a Reformulation of the Bott Hypothesis."

In *Network Analysis: Studies in Human Interaction.* edited by J. Boissevain and J.C. Mitchell. The Hague: Mouton.

Kitson, G.C. 1982. "Attachment to the Spouse in Divorce: A Scale and Its Application." *Journal of Marriage and the Family* 44: 379-393.

————. 1985. "Marital Discord and Marital Separation: A County Survey." *Journal of Marriage and the Family* 47: 693-700.

Kitson, G.C., and H.J. Raschke. 1981. "Divorce Research: What We Know; What We Need to Know." *Journal of Divorce* 4: 1-317.

Klimmer, D., and R. Kohl. 1984. *Fatherhood U.S.A.: The First Guide to Programs, Services, and Resources For and About Fathers.* New York: Guilford Press.

Kraus, S. 1979. "The Crisis of Divorce: Growth Promoting or Pathogenic?" *Journal of Divorce* 3: 107-119.

Kurdek, L.A., and D. Blisk. 1983. "Dimensions and Correlates of Mothers' Divorce Experiences." *Journal of Divorce* 6: 1-24.

Lamb, M.E. 1981. *The Role of the Father in Child Development.* New York: Wiley.

LaRossa, R., and J.H. Wolf. 1985. "On Qualitative Family Research." *Journal of Marriage and the Family* 47: 531-541.

Laumann, E.O. 1966. *Prestige and Association in an Urban Community.* Indianapolis: Bobbs-Merril.

Lee, G. 1979. "Effects of Social Networks on the Family." In *Contemporary Theories About the Family,* vol. 1, edited by W. Burr, R. Hill, F.I. Nye, and I. Reiss. New York: Basic Books.

Levine, J., J. Pleck, and M. Lamb. 1982. "The Fatherhood Project." In *Fatherhood and Social Policy,* edited by M. Lamb and A. Sagi. Hillsdale, NJ: Lawrence Erlbaum.

Levinger, G., and O. Moles. 1979. *Divorce and Separation: Context, Causes, and Consequences.* New York: Basic Books.

Lewis, B.A., and J.H. Pleck. 1979. "Special Issue on Men's Role in the Family." *Family Coordinator* 28: 4-6.

Luepnitz, D.A. 1982. *Child Custody. A Study of Families after Divorce.* Lexington, MA: D.C. Heath.

Lupri, E., and J. Frideres. 1981. "The Quality of Marriage and the Passage of Time: Marital Satisfaction Over the Family Life Cycle." *Canadian Journal of Sociology* 6: 283-305.

McCarthy, J. and J. Menken. 1978. "A Comparison of the Probability of the Dissolution of First and Second Marriages." *Demography* 15: 345-359.

McCormick, M. 1974. *Stepfathers: What the Literature Reveals.* La Jolla, CA: Western Behavioral Sciences Institute.

McGoldrick, M., and E.A. Carter. 1980. "Forming a Remarried Family." In *The Family Life Cycle: A Framework for Family Therapy,* edited by E.A. Carter and M. McGoldrick. New York: Gardner Press.

McKee, L., and M. O'Brien, eds. 1982. *The Father Figure.* London: Tavistock.

Maddox, B. 1975. *The Half Parent.* London: André Deutsch.

Mendes, H. A. 1976. "Single Fatherhood." *Social Work* 21: 308-312.

Messinger, L. 1976. "Remarriage Between Divorced People with Children from Previous Marriages: A Proposal for Preparation for Marriage." *Journal of Marriage and Family Counselling* 2: 193-200.

_____. 1984. *Remarriage: A Family Affair.* New York: Plenum.

Mueller, C. W., and H. Pope. 1977. "Marital Instability: A Study of its Transmission Between Generations." *Journal of Marriage and the Family* 39: 83-92.

_____. 1980. "Divorce and Female Remarriage Mobility: Data on Marriage Matches After Divorce for White Women." *Social Forces* 50: 726-738.

Murch, M. 1980. *Justice and Welfare in Divorce.* London: Sweet & Maxwell.

Nelson, G. 1981. "Moderators of Women's and Children's Adjustment Following Parental Divorce." *Journal of Divorce* 4: 71-83.

Newcombe, M.D. 1984. "Marital Discord and Problem Areas: Longitudinal Personality Prediction of Sex Differences Among the Divorced." *Journal of Divorce* 8: 67-77.

Niemeijer, R. 1973. "Some Applications of the Notion of Density to Network Analysis." In *Network Analysis, Studies in Human Interaction,* edited by J. Boissevain and J. C. Mitchell. The Hague: Mouton.

Noble, M. 1973. "Social Networks: Its Use as a Conceptual Framework in Family Analysis." In *Network Analysis,*

Studies in Human Interaction, edited by J. Boissevain and J. Clyde Mitchell. The Hague: Mouton.

Nolan, J.F. 1977. "The Impact of Divorce on Children." *Conciliation Courts Review* 15: 2-7.

Norton, A.J. 1977. "Family Life Cycle: 1980." *Journal of Marriage and the Family* 45: 267-275.

Norton, A.J., and P.C. Glick. 1976. "Marital Instability: Past, Present, and Future." *Journal of Social Issues* 32: 5-20.

Norton, R. 1983. "Measuring Marital Quality: A Critical Look at the Dependent Variable." *Journal of Marriage and the Family* 45: 141-151.

Nye, F.I., and F.M. Berardo. 1973. *The Family: Its Structure and Interaction.* New York: Macmillan.

Orthner, D.K., T. Brown, and D. Ferguson. 1976. "Single-parent Fatherhood: An Emerging Family Life Style." *Family Coordinator* 25: 429-437.

Perkins, T.F., and James P. Kahan. 1979. "An Empirical Comparison of Natural Father and Stepfather Family System." *Family Process* 18: 175-183.

Peters, J.F. 1979. "A Comparison of Mate Selection and Marriage in the First and Second Marriages in a Selected Sample of the Remarried Divorced." Pp. 419-426 in *Cross-Cultural Perspectives of Mate-Selection and Remarriage,* edited by G. Kurian. Wesport, CT: Greenwood Press.

Petronio, S. 1988. "Communication and the Visiting Parent." *Journal of Divorce* 11: 103-110.

Plateris, A. 1979. *Divorces by Marriage Cohort.* Hyattsville, MD: National Center for Health Statistics.

Pope, H., and C. W. Mueller. "The Intergenerational Transmission of Marital Instability: Comparisons by Race and Sex." *Journal of Social Issues* 32: 49-66.

Price-Bonham, S., and J.O. Balswick. 1980. "The Non Institutions: Divorce, Desertion, and Remarriage." *Journal of Marriage and the Family* 42: 959-972.

Rallings, E.M. 1976. "The Special Eole of the Stepfather." *Family Coordinator* 25: 445-449.

Reiss, D., and M.E. Oliveri. 1983. "The Family's Construction of Social Vality and Its Ties to Its Kin Network: An Exploration of Causal Direction." *Journal of Marriage and the Family* 45: 81-91.

Rettig, K., and M.M. Bubolz. 1983. "Interpersonal Resource Exchange as Indicators of Quality of Marriage." *Journal of Marriage and the Family* 45: 497-509.

Richards, M.P.M. 1982. "Post-divorce Arrangements for Children: A Psychological Perspective." *Journal of Social Welfare Law* 133-151.

Robinson, M. 1980. "Step-families: A Reconstituted Family System." *Journal of Family Therapy* 2: 45-69.

Rogler, L.H., and M.E. Procidano. 1989. "Marital Heterogamy and Marital Quality in Puerto Rican Families." *Journal of Marriage and the Family* 51: 363-372.

Rollins, B.C., and K.L. Cannon. 1974. "Marital Satisfaction Over the Family Life Cycle: A Reevaluation." *Journal of Marriage and the Family* 30: 271-282.

Rosenblum K.E. 1986. "Leaving As a Wife, Leaving As a Mother." *Journal of Family Issues* 7: 197-213.

Rosenthal, E. 1970. "Divorce and Religious Intermarriage: The Effect of Previous Marital Status Upon Subsequent Marital Behavior." *Journal of Marriage and the Family* 32: 435-440.

Rosenthal, K.M., and H.F. Keshet. 1981. *Fathers Without Partners.* Totowa, N.J.: Rowman & Littlefield.

Rossi, A.S. 1980. "Aging and Parenthood in the Middle Years. In *Life-Span Development and Behavior,* vol. 3, edited by P.B. Baltes and O.G. Brim. New York: Academic Press.

Russel, G., and N. Radin. 1983. "Increased Parental Participation: The Fathers' Perspective." In *Fatherhood and Family Policy,* edited by M.E. Lamb and A. Sagi. Hillsdale, NJ: Lawrence Erlbaum.

Safilios-Rothschild, C. 1969. "Family Sociology or Wives' Sociology? A Cross-cultural Examination of Decision-making." *Journal of Marriage and the Family* 31: 290-301.

Sanders, G.F., and D.W. Trygstad. 1989. "Stepgrandparents and Grandparents: The View From Young Adults." *Family Relations* 38: 71-75.

Santrock, J.W., and K.A. Sitterle. 1987. "Parent-Child Relationships in Stepmother Families." In *Remarriage and Stepparenting,* edited by K. Pasely and M. Ihinger-Tallman. New York: Guilford Press.

Santrock, J.W., R. Warshak, C. Lindbergh, and L. Meadows. 1982. "Children's and Parents' Observed Social Behavior in Stepfather Families." *Child Development* 53: 472-480.

Schlesinger, B. 1979. "Remarriage as Family Reorganization for Divorced Persons—A Canadian Study." Pp. 401-418 in *Cross-Cultural Perspectives of Mate-Selection and Remarriage*, edited by G. Kurian. Wesport, CT: Greenwood Press.

Singh, B.K., L.A. Adams, and D.E. Jorgenson. 1978. "Epidemiology of Marital Unhappiness." *International Journal of the Sociology of the Family* 8: 207-218.

Spanier, G.B. 1976. "Measuring Dyadic Adjustment: New Scales for Assessing the Quality of Marriage and Similar Dyads." *Journal of Marriage and the Family* 38: 15-28.

————. 1983. "Married and Unmarried Cohabitation in the United States: 1980." *Journal of Marriage and the Family* 45: 277-288.

Spanier, G.B., and P. Glick. 1980. "Paths to Remarriage." *Journal of Divorce* 3: 283-298.

Spanier, G.B., and R. Lewis. 1980. "Marital Quality: A Review of the Seventies." *Journal of Marriage and the Family* 42: 825-839.

Spanier, G.B., R.A. Lewis, and C.L. Cole. 1975. "Marital Adjustment Over the Family Life Cycle: The Issue of Curvilinearity." *Journal of Marriage and the Family* 31: 263-268.

Spanier, G.B., and L. Thompson. 1984. *Parting: The Aftermath of Separation and Divorce*. Beverly Hills, CA: Sage.

Sprey, J. 1985. "Editorial Comments." *Journal of Marriage and the Family*. 47: 523.

Statistics Canada. 1981. *Vital Statistics*. Vol. 2: *Marriages and Divorces*. Ottawa: Statistics Canada.

Stein, P.J. 1984. "Men in Families." *Marriage and Family Review* 7: 143-162.

Steinberg, L., and S.B. Silverberg. 1987. "Influences on Marital Satisfaction During the Middle Stages of the Family Life Cycle." *Journal of Marriage and the Family* 49: 751-760.

Stern, P.N. 1978. "Stepfather Families: Integration Around Child Discipline." *Issues in Mental Health Nursing* 1: 50-56.

Szinovacz, M. 1983. "Using Couple Data as a Methodological Tool: The Case of Marital Violence." *Journal of Marriage and the Family* 45: 613-644.

Thibaut, J.W. and H.H. Kelly. 1959. *The Social Psychology of Groups*. New York: Wiley.

Thompson, L., and A.J. Walker. 1982. "The Dyad as a Unit of Analysis: Conceptual and Methodological Issues." *Journal of Marriage and the Family* 44: 889-900.

Thomson, E., and R. Williams. 1982. "Beyond Wives' Family Sociology: A Method for Analyzing Couple Data." *Journal of Marriage and the Family* 44: 999-1008.

Tolsdorf, C.C. 1976. "Social Networks, Support and Coping: An Exploratory Study." *Family Process* 15: 407-418.

Turner, C. 1967. "Conjugal Roles and Social Networks: A Reexamination of an Hypothesis." *Human Relations* 20: 121-130.

U.S. Bureau of the Census. 1977. *Marriage, Divorce, Widowhood, and Remarriage by Family Characteristics: June 1975*. Current Population Reports, Series P. 20, no. 312. Washington, DC: U.S. Government Printing Office.

Udry, J. R. and M. Hall. 1965. "Marital Role Segregation and Social Networks in Middle-class Middle-aged Couples." *Journal of Marriage and the Family* 27: 392-395.

Vera, H., D.H. Berardo, and F.M. Berardo. 1985. "Age Heterogamy in Marriage." *Journal of Marriage and the Family* 47: 553-566.

Veroff, J., R.A. Kulka, and E. Douvan. 1981. *Mental Health in America: Patterns of Help-Seeking From 1957 to 1976*. New York: Basic Books.

Verbrugge, L.M. 1977. "The Structure of Adult Friendship Choices." *Social Forces* 56: 576-597.

Visher, E.B., and J.S. Visher. 1979. *Stepfamilies: A Guide to Working with Stepparents and Stepchildren*. New York: Brunner/Mazel.

————. 1982. *Step-families: Myths and Realities*. New York: Brunner/Mazel.

Walker, K. and L. Messinger. 1979. "Remarriage after Divorce: Dissolution and Reconstruction of Family Boundaries." *Family Process* 18: 185-192.

Wallerstein, J.S. 1988. "Women After Divorce: Preliminary Report From a Ten-Year Follow-Up." *American Journal of Orthopsychiatry* 56: 65-77.

Wallerstein, J.S., and J.B. Kelly. 1980. *Surviving the Breakup*. New York: Basic Books.

Weishaus, S., and D. Field. 1985. "A Half Century of Marriage: Continuity or Change?" *Journal of Marriage and the Family* 50: 763-773.

Weitzman, L.J. 1985. *The Divorce Revolution: The Unexpected Social and Economic Consequences for Women and Children in America*. New York: The Free Press.

White, L. K. 1979. "Sex Differentials in the Effect of Remarriages on Global Happiness." *Journal of Marriage and the Family* 41: 869-876.

White, L.K. and A. Booth. 1985. "The Quality and Stability of Remarriages: The Role of Stepchildren." *American Sociological Review* 50: 689-698.

White, L.K. and D. Brinkerhoff. 1978. "Measuring Dyadic Properties: An Exploratory Analysis." *International Journal of the Sociology of the Family* 8: 219-229.

White, L.K., D.B. Brinkerhoff, and A. Booth. 1985. "The Effects of Marital Disruption on Child's Attachment to Parents." *Journal of Family Issues* 6: 5-22.

White, S.W., and K. Mika. 1983. "Family Divorce and Separation: Theory and Research." *Journal of Divorce* 6: 175-192.

Whiteside, M.F. 1989. "Family Rituals As a Key to Kinship Connections in Remarried Families." *Family Relations* 38: 34-39.

Wilson, K.L., L.A. Zurcher, D.C. McAdams, and R.C. Curtis. 1975. "Stepfathers and Stepchildren: An Exploratory Analysis from Two National Surveys." *Journal of Marriage and the Family*. 37: 526-536.

Wimberly, H. 1973. "Conjugal-role Organization and Social Networks in Japan and England." *Journal of Marriage and the Family* 35: 125-131.

Author Index

Subject Index